COGGERS

By

Norman Shaw

All EVPs available at

www.ahauntedlife.com

Map of Coggers

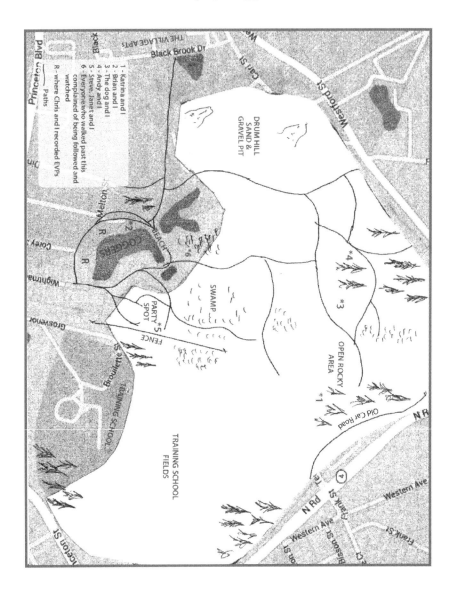

Christyann, there is a wonderful world that exists alongside ours. I hope this gives you a glimpse into that. Remember that fear is afraid of one thing, love. So always try to hold it in your heart.

Keep Shining

This book is the work of a large amount of effort, not only mine, but others as well. Some of my friends patiently read its first version and gave me polite criticism; others couldn't get through the first draft and were too polite to tell me. Re-reading it, I slowly came to realize how bad it was and how very blessed I was with kind people in my life. So I re-wrote it, and then again and again and again. Till I produced this version, which I hope you enjoy. Here is a partial list of helpers/contributors and general well wishers who inspired me at some point. Thanks to Michelle
Brown, Bill Laforme, Richard Dixon, Tonya Dahlhaus, Shona Kier, Dennis Rudy at the gym who kept asking, "When is your book comingout?", and so many others

Of course, thanks to Chris Wood for heading down there with me and taking a psychic beating so very many times. Great thanks go to Michelle Blais, who helped design so many of the wonderful things you see, as well as the website.

Thanks also go to the spirits of Coggers who chose to give us their names, this book is because of you Bobbi, Vincent, Edna, James, Mary Menkham, Gus and Heath, it's because of you guys that I wrote the book and I hope your aware I pray for you every night as I promised. I know you know.

This life is more magical and wonderful than we could ever believe. I hope that my journey shows you an example of that.

Norman Shaw, 2/2014

PREFACE by Chris Wood

Norm Shaw... heh... when I say his name, it makes me smile, because that's how I always feel in his company, happy. Here is a man that has been to hell and back and come out smiling. An admirable feat for anyone. I was introduced to this man by a shamanic teacher. Being a 'seeker of truth' and a lover of the metaphysical, I often would find meditation groups and white witches. Since I had now moved across the pond, the Witches of the UK had been replaced by the Shamans of the Americas. This time I had found a warm-hearted man, with an obvious confidence and a good knowledge of the unseen. I asked him if he would take me on as a student, as I knew he could help me along my own path with a little guidance. He said he had his hands full right now, but he knew someone who would be just perfect for me to meet. So it was arranged, he told me of this man, a few years older than myself that would come along to their 'investigations'. (Where they would go out, as a group, into the neighborhoods of Massachusetts and New Hampshire and help people with hauntings). "Storming Norman!" he would call him with a laugh and a certain amount of admiration. It certainly helped to peak my curiosity.

"Why is he 'Stormin'?" I asked with a smirk and a wink. "Well, whenever we go to a haunted space, he always asked where the most haunted area was. Then he would charge in there, sit right in the thick of the darkest, heaviest energy and meditate."

Storming indeed! This guy seemed fearless! How could anyone say no to this kind, thoughtful introduction? The day we were to meet was on a much bigger investigation. It was open to the public and this small group had organized going into an old mill building somewhere in Mass. I was impressed with the gathering, only expecting around 25 people, there must've been about double that turn up. Everyone had a similar idea in mind, to explore and feel out a haunted space. It had become quite an exciting thing to do, popularized by television now, it was, (dare I say it?), fashionable. The night started with us all meeting in an old cafe room I think it was. All the seats were taken and people continued to pour in. I met with the shamans, who I had met earlier and looked around for this mysterious Norm character. I imagined I would know who it would be, trying to trust my instincts. I can't imagine how many people I labeled as Norm that night in my excitement to meet this spiritual warrior. Which is quite funny now that I look back and reflect on it, how excited I was and how new and fascinating all the metaphysicalwas to me back then. I was still terrified of it all, but felt safe within the group.

I'm not exactly sure how it happened or how we met now, but I remember walkingalong with him outside as we walked towards one of the haunted buildings. I felt like I had known him for ages, always a great feeling when you meet a stranger. There was an instant level of comfort and ease of talking. He was tall and had a face that seemed to be constantly smiling. Later I would learn he had a penchant for comedy and would pester me about Monty Python as he knew I was British. Iwould continually tell him that it was 50 years old now. But he always continued, he won the day, as he always does, with his playful persistence. Now we joke about it often, something I found so 'passe' in my youthful arrogance had now been returned to just being something fun. His penchant for comedy went further when I learned that he and a group of friends that wrote skits together and he would share some of them with me. Some of them were really good too, and I'm a tough one to tickle. He is also a father, it's in his demeanor. The way he talks and acts, he's a dad, anyone can see that. So as I was his pupil to a degree, he was another father figure to me for a time. After seeing Norm charge the darkest regions of the mill with his sword of courage waving above his head, riding on his steed of willful determination and shouting cries of "I fear thee not!" I knew this guy was going to be a lot of fun to hang out with.

So it was we started to meet every week. I was an hours drive south of him at the time, in the Framingham area of Mass. We'd meet on Friday nights and he'd take me to this devilish area in his home town. I feel like back then I was merely a boy, I was still looking for father figures to guide me and I was new to America. AlsoI was new to marriage, everything was new, my new life in the new world had started. I was just a boy and I had a lot to learn and more importantly, re-learn. He would tell me how he was unimpressed with his nights out with the ghost group,because where he grew up there were hauntings so tangible and real that it made everything pale by comparison. I thought he might be trying to build this magical place up. Like a lot of peopledo to make their stories more exciting and larger than life. When you read the book you will understand what I mean. His tales really are larger than life and it took me a while to realize that he wasn't joking when he said this place was haunted. Back then I felt like I was a new world arrival, a little lost and confused, asking at tourist information for a map of the area. Luckily at this time, Norman Shaw was at the front desk, dressed in fullplate mail, with a broadsword tied to his hip and his horse tied up outside. "I'll show you around the darkest areas in Chelmsford young knave! You have nothing to fear when Sir Norman is by your side!"He just always appears as a knight of the middle ages in my eyes, bold and courageous, filled with honor, (although you may not believe it from his rambunctious youth), and also with pride and confidence. So there we are, another night down in the darkness of Coggers. This is the place where I learnt to put my fear of the unseen to one side and replace it with compassion and understanding, all under the tutelage of Sir Norman of Shaw.

It generally went like this: we'd meet at a popular coffee shop, grab a big cup each, (which he would pay for more often than not out of kindness for his temporarily out of work friend, caught between the rock of "post 2008"and the hard place of attaining a Green Card). Then he'd drive us down to the woods. We'd tool up with smudge, feathers, voice recorders and sometimes cameras and of course, the coffee. In the winter we'd build a fire to keep warm. We also both knew that fire is multi dimensional and if you think about this and picture it; it feels like it's almost more in some other dimension than this one! (Yes, I have no scientific backing here, just an imaginative mind, another important tool). We'd go down the steep banks, normally to the same spot, and sit by the water and just chat about anything and everything. We'd have a laugh; it'd be like going to the pub for a drink with my mates back home. But this had a few extra twists, because after a while, strange things would happen. Now as I type this out, I'm only on chapter 10 of his book. I haven't got to thebit where he and I are hanging out together every week. So I'm not sure I want to go into it deeply, this is after all his book and this part is only the preface. It's really meant to introduce the man behind the book. So I won't recount those experiences here. But I had enough to amaze myself into submission to my, then shaky, beliefs. We had EVPs that made absolutely EVERYTHING I had seen on telly look just plain by comparison. That felt pretty good. Once the EVPs started responding to us, then it got even more astounding and it was at about that time that Norman realized he really had to write the book.

After a while I wasn't 'new born in the new world' anymore. I was just another dude in America, with a peculiar accent. We started working down Coggers together. Clearing the darkness of the place and doing what we thought was right to help the trapped spirits down there. Whilst we may have been a little blind back then, our hearts were open and our intentions were good. Then one fateful day, he did me the great honor of saying, "I've learnt at least as much from you as you have learnt from me". This was a turning point, because normally when I meet these teachers there is often an air of arrogance. It's the old "I'm more spiritual than you" feeling you get from meeting in these groups. I know I played along, everyone believed in themselves. You have to really, if you're going to let a little 'weird' into your life. So at this point, I realized, this was not just a teacher, it was a friend. And from then on, that is what we became, learning from each other and helping each other out, as friends do.

To this day he is still then only guy in America I can honestly label as a friend. I am not one to make many and the ones I do make, stay with me for life. I am honored to call Norm Shaw one of them, and I thank him for all his teachings and his continual wisdom even to this day

Chris Wood.

I, as the author, would like to point out that I didn't pay Chris much money for that preface.

PREFACE

Hey there, thanks for buying and taking time to read this part of the book. Personally I always skipped the introductions because I just wanted to get to the story. As a writer, I think maybe I should go through my library once more and see what my favorite authors have to say about their projects. Because now, I realize that's what this part is for. It is a "holy crap, thank God I am done," part of the book, and also a good time to vent and let a sigh of relief. This was a lot like my journey itself, full of twists and turns and many, many unpleasant surprises. Far from being a natural writer, all my witticisms ended up falling flat and I found that like any talent, ability comes with experience. More importantly to me, it took me a long time to figure out what to call this book.

>Coggers,
>Say it out loud
>Coggers,
>Coggers
>Say it one more time please
>Coggers,

Coggers, the name of the woods themselves, isn't a word that rolls off the tongue easily. It's foreign sounding, slightly harsh on the roof of your mouth and as I sit here typing and saying it over and over. I am reminded of oil for some reason, a great big greasy slick of black oil. All in all, Coggers is a perfect description of the place itself. Hence the name, as you read, I know that even the most open minded will have beliefs called into to question. That's good, it's good to have our comfort zone shaken once in awhile. Let me say outright that everything in this book is completely true. It all happened in the manner described, to the best of my ability to remember anyway. I am not here trying to convince anyone of anything. You either believe or you don't. Personally, my whole life has been far too extraordinary for me to feel the need to embellish, (at least I think so). You can accept my story and my lessons and learn from them or not. Always, every moment we exercise creations perfect gift, choice. I see no purpose in lying.

Some of the people's names have been changed, in other cases, not. This is a true story and these are real people, Coggers is real, and if you were so inclined, you could go there and collect EVP's and sense for yourself. I would recommend against it. Please don't. Let me say that one more time, in bold and italics, so that you get the point. ***Seriously, don't go there*** It is filled with dark energy and while some serious spiritual work remains to be done, I don't recommend you do it. Some would say that it is wrong of me, to try and keep them there, or prevent others from clearing the space. Well, that's your opinion, and in all honesty, I suggest you read this book before you even attempt at "crossing a spirit" again because chances are, you aren't doing what you think you are doing. Let me make one more effort into knocking some sense into you by saying, "there is something there that wants you to come." Much like a shark would want a 400lb bag of blubber, there is something there waiting for you, so please DO NOT GO THERE.

Lastly, this book is meant to be read while listening to the EVP's **(www.ahauntedlife.com)**. They go hand and hand, if you read the book and don't listen to them, it will fall flat. It is much the same as just going to the website and listening to the files without reading the book, they are a part of one another, so please listen to them as the book cues them up for you. You have no idea the energy physical and psychic that went into getting them.

CHAPTER 1

It was one of those rare New England nights, it wasn't hot and I didn't need my coat, just perfectto sit there in the sand, on the hillside next to the pond. I took a deep breath in and enjoyed that warm primordial swampy smell. I always associated it with Coggers, and whiffing it, brought back a thousand different memories from my childhood. The crickets were chirping the temperature off and the bullfrogs' chorus was growing louder. Occasionally, a bass would jump; searching for a nighttime snack and the pond's beaver could be seen silently cruising the surface, slapping his tail from time to time. Chris and Dave were talking about something next to me, but I wasn't paying attention. I was focused on what I was feeling around me as I took another deep breath and began to meditate. I ignored the mosquitoes as they buzzed my ears and started running energy through myself.

After an indeterminate amount of time, when I had finished, I gathered all my energy up into a ball that I could feel and I willed it out with a giant, "It's me!" of intention attached to it. I knew the woods, the pond, the area, and it all knew me - and

I knew they remembered me. If whatever was down there was around, it was going to sense what I just did. I turned towards my friends in the pale moonlight, my neck popping and said, "Wait half an hour, something will happen." They just shrugged and since I was speaking again, added me to their conversation. As we sat around on the ground, talking and laughing, feeling the cold spots sway in among us, Again, I marveled at the night, it really was perfect out. Once and a while someone would give a loud"whoa," as a chill ran through them or laugh when Dave ripped a loud fart. We were just a bunch of guys hanging out, sensing the spirits around us, being goofy and laughing.

That's what we were doing there, on that beautiful New England night, trying to pick up on the spirit world. We were sitting in the most haunted place in North America doing it. While you might argue with me over this and bring up other locations you have heard or read about, Coggers was the real deal. It wasn't a story that started with, "this one place, I heard of."No, we were here and nowhere had I known of, or read about, did the other side punch through like it did in Coggers. This is what we were doing there that night, trying to get it to come through again. Stupid, I know.

We could have long, awkward conversations about why I was in haunted woods, meditating and trying to get the spirit world to come through. Some of you would shake your head and think I was nuts, others might wonder if I was evil. I will get to that, for now, just bear with me as this tale meanders about. You see, a few weeks before, I had begun seeing things. Yes, "seeing things," When I say that to people, I always get a funny look and imagine themthinking of LSD flashbacks or some poor wino with the DT's having hallucinations. This wasn't anything likethat; it was something amazing, almost magical, in its oddity. It had first started when I was investigating a haunted house with a ghost group I was in. I had seen what looked like a round swatch of someone's flannel shirt moving across the room. Imagine for a moment, standing in a living room of someone's house and seeing a ball of red light with white stripes whipping across a room at knee level. Think for a moment of how that might affect your psyche. The first thing you think of is TUMOR, especially when no one else with you sees it. Then you start seeing pillars of smoke in various locations about your room when coming out of meditation, or even shimmering waves of energy, irregularly shaped.

MRI anyone?

Suffice to say, I had gone from living life as a normal guy, (really my friend, what is normal?), to staring around rooms like a cat. Friends would look over their shoulders to see what I was looking at, or stare at where I was, trying to see what I was focused on. So sometimes I would see what looked like smoke, or balls of light, and sometimes energy.
What the hell is energy?
What do you mean you see things?

Well, the easiest way to describe it is if you remember on Star Trek, when they beamed people up? Take out the blue light and that's what I would see, behind people, standing next to them, in corners, in stores, everywhere! In the fuckingbathroom on occasion, like seriously, if you're going to spend the afterlife somewhere, pick a better place than the john ok? But really, once I began to accept it, it became fascinating to me. It took quite awhile to get used to it, at least to the point where I didn't react when I noticed a spirit. I can see your raised eyebrows from here, don't ask me, I am a concrete guy and I make my money the hard way. It was only in the last few years that I had embarked on the most amazing journey, after being healed by the divine.

But I get off track and ahead of myself.

Like I said, I had been seeing things for a while now, and down in the woods it was a little bit more than usual. Sometimes it was somebody standing on my side, then turning and no one was there, (not a quick shadow like we all do, but a full person standing there). Sometimes I would see little wisps of smoke, or energy, or whatever what you want to call it, dancing about. Dave, Chris and I had been in Coggers for about an hour or so. We had felt and sensed more in that time than most people do in their whole lives.

That night, Chris and I had looked at each other after we saw leaves rustling down the hill in a straight line, and right in between us. He looked at me, and while fully believing in the spirit world, asked, "Do you think there's a frog under there or something?" Shortly after, Dave and I had heard what sounded like something knocking trees over near the old reform school. A very heavy falling sound, literally, like a giant was pushing trees over. Add to that a hundred crunchy footsteps in the gravel around us and that was our night so far. In that quick hour, we had heard and seen more than any TV show ghost hunting would in a month. That was Coggers, a truly haunted place.

Since my friends were just as nutty as me, they weren't surprised when I said, "I'm going to meditate for a bit," and didn't bother me like any normal human would. They let me sit in relative peace, gently lowering their voices. I sent my energy out (my power and intention around me), and released it with, "ITS ME!" knowing full well that the woods knew me. Knowing full well, that maybe whatever had chased me out as a kid all those times would come out and say, "Boo."

What a moron I was.

So there we sat, occasionally getting up, stretching our legs, good friends, swapping stories and enjoying each other's company. I was telling Dave about a friend of mine on the West Coast and how we had an offensive baseball rivalry going on when I heard something. Now whatever it was, to the ear, it sounded like an animal or a bird, the recorder picked it up clearer when it recorded **"you bastard" (more on that later) PLAY YOU BASTARD EVP**

"Did I just hear a raven, David, or a crow?" I asked. "I heard something faint," Chris said "something with attitude**, ber**".

It was nighttime and we were hearing a crow. Sitting there and looking up towards the sky, I had seen something black fly overhead. A wispy amorphous shape, nothing clearly defined, morelike a puff of black smoke, but moving.

"Did you hear it?" Dave asked.

"Sounded like a bird, quick, mep," Chris said.

"It sounded like something screamed," I told him.

"It could've been that sonar noise we heard." Mentioning a sound that Chris and I had heard a week prior.

"Interesting," Dave replied laconically.

"David just wait," I laughed, "bear with us another half hour or so."

"Not a problem," he replied.

"You gotta understand that you, Chris and I are a lot of light that's not normally seen down here. Did you hear that crow?"

"Yeah."

"I've never heard a crow at night before." I paused thoughtfully. "Interesting." "One of the first things I ever read," I paused. "Well, when I was in my 20s I had a dream of a man standing on rocks in the desert and he said, "Carlos Castaneda" so I started reading Carlos books, and the first thing that struck me was Don Juan saying that spirits can mimic animals, but imperfectly."

"Mmmm – hmmm," Dave replied.

"As I said it, I can feel it," I told him.

We talked for a bit longer, about spiritual things, about the signs that nature gives us, about everything under the sun.

"But still, even when this place goes off, when the energy is just right or what and the vortex cranks open or the portal opens, I have been down here, scared shitless, like, "What the fuck is that?" I said. I've met my neighbors in the morning and asked them, "What the hell is that?" and they are like "I don't know."

Yes, I did talk that way and say, "like, "every fifth word back then. We sat and talked and laughed and observed, then I felt something down there, "Yeah I know you're there, why don't you come over here, we're comfortable here," I said. "He'sgetting mad at me for saying that."

WHEN WE HEARD IT.
PLAY REAH EVP

In one noise, this thing brought me back to when I was a 10 year-old kid, being chased out of the woods, running for my life. I had been telling my ghost group friends, "Come with me to the woods, instead of this, I think I sense I feel, stuff, when this thing comes out, you're gonna say "What the fuckis that?" Well, none of the group had wanted to come, and here I was and here it was, shit. Chris's first words were "What the fuck was that?"

"A raven," Dave replied. Thinking of the raven he had heard earlier.

I knew what it was. I knew exactly what it was, and it took a lot of effort not to run right up the hill and say, "Screw you guys, I'm getting out of here."Years of memories of me and the woods flooded back, and it took all my will not to flee.

"Reah!" it screamed.

"Pheeewwwwwwwah," Chris whistled.

"Reah!"

I stood up and my first thought was, "Ah shit it's really here." I looked at where I heard it from, and couldn't see anything. It was less than ten feet away and invisible!

"Hello my friend, come down, are we bothering you?" asked Dave.

"Reah!" it screamed again. I stood up and held the recorder out and since it was voice activated, I could see the little red light on, it was rolling.

"Are you the mountain spirit? What do you wish to tell us?" Dave asked.

"Reah!" it screamed.

"Hi," Dave replied.

"Reah" it answered back.

"Come on."

"Reah"

"Reah"

"We're here to help. Guide us," Dave answered calmly.

"Show us how we can help you," I finally chimed in, and while not calm, I had gotten rid of some of that fear.

"Rehelp," it answered.

THE FRICKEN THING MIMICED ME

"Hello," Dave said, and the beaver slapped its tail on the water behind us, making a big splash and forcing my attention from whatever it was, to make sure nothing was coming out of the water to eat us.

"Reah," it said again, and I looked down and noticed the red light was off, and though this thing was screaming at us from ten feet away and was louder than our voices, it wasn't activating the recorder, I whistled to get it rolling again.

"You want to check us out? I think it's gone," Dave said. "It's still there, don't doubt it for a second."I shakily replied.
 As I looked around trying to see it, I noticed a series of red flashes at the top of the hill, like a car with red headlights was on the street, flicking them on and off. The beaver slapped its tail on the water again, diverting my attention that way. I looked back.

"We come in peace, we've come to help you," I said, trying to get the fear from my voice.

"You come through as a raven," Dave murmured.

"Damn beaver," I said as it slapped its tail behind us.

The recorder died again, and I whistled.

"That's a big flash," Chris laughed as he pointed up the hill.

"Reah," it said, this time some distance away.

"Hello," Dave answered.

"Damn beaver," I said to Chris since the beaver had just splashed behind us and made me turn again, I was jumpy. Then I pointed, "The flashes have moved from over there, to up there." I swept my arm farther down the trail.

"Yeah and it's really big, it looks like fire," he agreed.

"What shapes it shifted…" Dave started to say.

"Reah," it replied from off in the woods, even though it sounded hundreds of feet away. We hadn't heard one leaf, one stick, or even one pebble move.

"Reah"

"We've come to help." I sounded more confident now that it was farther away.

"My heart is open, to see the truth."

"Reah"

"Reah!" It was screaming at us as it moved around the pond, like we could actually hear its voice going farther and farther away, well not its voice, whatever it had, that passed as a voice.

The stupid beaver slapped its tail again, and the damn recorder wouldn't keep rolling. I had to constantly make noise to get it going.

I burped.

"Can you hear that?" Chris asked.

"Reah." It was on the other side of the pond.

"Reah"

"Is there a button for continuous record?" I asked Dave.

"I don't know," he replied.

"Reah"

"Welcome to the woods David."

And that was it. In those eight minutes we had stood our ground, and chased off the spirit/elemental/demon that haunted Coggers Pond for as long as I could remember.

I had come far from the child I used to be.

CHAPTER 2

I grew up on a dead end street in Lowell, Massachusetts. Whenever I saw that, "DEAD END" sign, I would think about the implications of it. What the hell did it mean? Was everyone's life here a dead end? Was everyone without a future? You know the type of thoughts that run through your head as a kid. Given my relative self-esteem as a child, I am not surprised that I thought this way. My parents lived near the DEAD END (another sign of my lack of future!) and the city property line ran right through their house. When I say the city line went through the house, I mean literally, the city property line went through the house. I slept in Lowell and ate breakfast in Chelmsford. As a kid I always had plans to use that to my advantage should the need ever arise.

"You see your honor, the city of the Lowell made the arrest in the side of the house in Chelmsford, therefore our client, the dread pirate Norman must be released."
"Case dismissed!"

You get the idea. I was lucky in some ways as a child, growing up in Lowell, which had been an industrial city for over 100 years, I had 40-plus acres of woods near my parents' house. For a while, when I was young, there was an active gravel pit down there, and because we were stupid, we used to run among the machinery, dodging dump trucks, accompanied by the musical,"get the fuck out of here you stupid kids!" shouts of the drivers and workers.On the weekends we had free run of the place and climbed EVERYTHING, broke anything breakable and generally looked for trouble. Sometimes we scaled the mountain-sized piles of sand and would pretend to ski down, jumping from side to side. Grabbing handfuls of rocks, we would throw them at anything within range, animate, inanimate and sometimes each other. The fact that we never died during our brilliant, "let's dig a tunnel into the side of this giant pile of sand," phase is a testament to the kindness of natural selection in my area. Once in awhile during the week we would be bold and stop in the gravel company's office and get a drink from the water cooler during our cut-thru's to Drum Hill and beyond. But Coggers, the rest that didn't have dump trucks and loaders crawling over it, was awesome. The woods had every kind of terrain, from swamp to pine forest, to desert and lush vegetation and a stinky pond that was great fishing.

There was also a dump in my neighborhood that everyone used. It was as the 1970's after all, and no one would understand the words, "global warming," combined in sentence form. As kids, my friends and I would go down to the dump and sift through the discards of the neighborhood, (dirty books dirty books, come on dirty books), and collect bottles to break in the sand pits near the end of Wightman Street. Collecting them and returning them for money wasn't nearly as rewarding as flying glass and the musical sound of breaking that accompanied a good shot. Down in Coggers we played army men, (always Generals, always killing the Nazi hordes), built fires, fished, pretended to hunt and basically got filthy dirty everyday. It was a magical place to grow up. I think I was about ten when my mom finally gave me permission to actually go to the woods. I had been sneaking down there for years, with the older kids, (and alone), but now, I didn't have to lie when she asked me where I had been.

As a child of the 70's, I had been out and about exploring the five or six square miles that comprised my world since I was old enough to walk. Those were great times to be a kid. It seemed there were always other children around, either a year older or a year younger, ready to play army, to explore or to just generally cause trouble. Not like now, where I see rusty bikes and tumbleweeds rolling down streets, while computer screens glow out of windows. When I was a kid, there were always scratch street hockey and football games being played. Even on the rainiest, most miserable day, you know if you knocked on enough doors, you would come to someone whose parents were sick of them and wanted them out of the house. In my neighborhood, we would march to someone's door, knock and yell out their name in a long drawn out version of a kid doorbell, "Terrrrrrryyyyyy" or "Errrrrriiiicc," and then usually an adult would come and announce the child's presence or lack thereof. For some strange reason though, knocking alone never seemed to work. One could bloody their knuckles on a door, and no one would come, but yelling the name, that got results. Never once in my childhood did a parent come to the door and say, "what the hell are you doing out here, yelling my sons name like that???" It was just a thing of my neighborhood.

Back then, parents were something to be avoided at all costs if possible. Enforcers of the law, they often meted out punishment, cancelled play dates, (though, in my neighborhood, if you said "play date" you would've been beaten up), and sent you home when you and your friend got caught doing something you shouldn't have been or worse, called your parents for your own beating when you returned. There were no "Cool parents "like now, only "shit, it's my parents," parents.

    Usually I would get kicked out of the house after doing my chores, "get some fresh air," or "go outside it's beautiful out."It didn't matter if we were caught in a Nor'easter or if hail was coming down, anything that would remove my sulky face from my parents' gaze was something to be acted upon by them.

    "Be back at lunch," my mom would yell as I headed out, or, "don't be late for dinner." I would already be scrambling my sneakers on to leave before they changed their mind, and my stepdad gave me more chores to do. Armed with my trusty Timex, I would march out and go around and knock on doors, looking for friends to do something with. As I think of it now, I am amazed that none of us ever got kidnapped or abducted. (Though I swear my mom used to tell me to take candy from strangers or free rides.) I guess their rationale was, "well if we lose one or two, what does it matter, we have more or can have more and maybe the new ones won't be as screwed up as this bunch."

    Whatever the reason, my parents wanted to be left alone and would send me out the moment my indentured servitude was over for the day. Even better, since I was so tricky and deceitful, I would wind my watch back an hour when we were in the middle of a kickball game or playing relieve e o, then I'd walk in and say, "I think my watch is broken," with a blank innocent look on my face. When they yelled, err, asked why I was late, never once did anyone let on how stupid I was. As the third child, all the excuses had been used and I could seldom pull a fast one on them.Don't think it was just my parents wanting to be left alone by sending me out into the world. All my friends' parents would get sick of our chatter and say, "get out of here," or "why don't you go outside?" and we would be cast into the bright world, "Andy has some things to do," when they only tired of my voice and sent me back into the streets to wander and start banging on other peoples doors.

So my street was a DEAD END. It had rows of middle class houses lining each side. Behind them were their backyards, neatly fenced off, and behind those, were the backyards of the houses on the next street. I knew every property in the neighborhood, probably better than the owners themselves. Those fences made easy climbing and I explored and nosed about everyone's yard like it was my own. This arrangement of houses on DEAD END streets ran on until it hit the Training school on one side and a swampy part of Coggers on the other. My street was bisected by Princeton Boulevard and there were another six houses on the upper half of Corey Street (eight now, as building regulations have been relaxed).My neighbors were unlike anything I've encountered to this day. From the "candy lady," whose door we knocked on once a day to get nasty sugar coated jelly slices, to Mr. Thomas local cop, whose children were older and bought us beer as teenagers. We knew them and they knew us, and I don't remember anyone saying, "Get your skinny ass out of my yard kid!" Usually it was, "Norman, what are you doing there?" to which I would exchange pleasantries and then continue on my way of exploring someone else's property.

If you were so inclined to continue on, the other half of my street continued into a smallish swamp smack dab in the middle of about three dead end streets. I think we were about 12 years old when some parent yelled out, "you kids get the hell out of there... that's septic water! Busy playing with the little rivulets, we thought the pretty brown water was interesting, something to dam up as it leached into the soil. (Did I mention natural selection was kind in my neighborhood?) Through this swamp, to another short dead end road you came out onto Middlesex Street. Busier, this was usually bustling with cars and trucks and we learned at a young age to look both ways before crossing. There are few things like a couple of close calls with death to make you more aware of traffic and your surroundings in general.

Taking a left onto Middlesex Street, after a couple of houses, you were struck by a cluster of brick buildings known as the Chariot Apartments. These were large apartment houses clustered around a pool and a parking area (the tight spaces behind the buildings were perfect for playing war in and spying into the first floor windows). Across the street from the Chariot apartments was Dusobox, a large mysterious wooden building, surrounded by barbed wire fencing. It was forbidding and forlorn, its multi pane windows with cardboard squares over the missing glass, its wooden sides painted steel grey. We didn't know what went on in there and we didn't want to know, (for the most part). Once we found a case of Diet 7 Up in the dumpster there on a hot summer day. After inspection and an Algonquin round table discussion of why they would throw it out, the labeling of, "it contained saccharine which was reputedly able to cause cancer in laboratory animals," we shrugged and proceeded to drink it.

I think of it now, 11 year old kids, drinking soda they had taken from a dumpster of a mysterious building and I have to laugh. Anyway, behind Dusobox ran the railroad tracks, all the way down from New Hampshire, along the Merrimack River, all the way into Lowell and beyond.

As I said, my neighborhood was great. Always one level of exploration followed by another and ad infinitum. For the most part, around me was Coggers and middle class homes, but the farther you got into Lowell, the more apartment buildings and the more violent the kids were there. Them and their friendly greetings of, "what the fuck are you looking at?" We tended to stay close to home and avoid strangers. Why not? When you got bored, you could always bang on someone's door and holler their name out hoping they were around to explore it with you.

Coggers is in the opposite direction, less than 100 feet from my parents' driveway. All you could see was leaves, a path and a small hilltop. There was brush everywhere, so the paths through it were clearly defined. Even among the brush there were strands of long yellow grass that poked up for most of the year. Then it was covered with a thick carpet of oak leaves in the fall. Everywhere was life, and everywhere life fought its tenacious hold. I loved it, and as kids we tried to kill as much of it as possible. I always see it, in my mind's eye, how it looked then, standing there in front of the house, looking towards it, like I've done hundreds of thousands of times. The hill, with its heavy canopy of tree cover and the clear sand paths that abounded there, the odd one tree trying to grow out to the light, brushes clawing their way upward, and always the constant chatter of life in motion. All day long, birds flitted from limb to limb, squirrels bounced along doing their stupid squirrel things, and sometimes you would glimpse a fox or raccoons running away from you. In the middle of blazing hot summer days, you would hear the long drawn out buzzing of cicadas baking in the heat. From my driveway, walking towards Coggers, there were large paths on either side at the base of the hill. When I was real young, when I wasn't supposed to be down there, these paths were large enough to take cars down. Blocked off with rocks and starting to grow in by the time I was 12. They led to the streets on either side of mine, and at night I could clearly hear the teenagers parked in their cars, drinking beer, down there. It was so much easier to cut through than walk to the end of the street and then down. As you walked up into Cogs, (as we called it), you climbed up a small hill with trees on top. This knoll roughly extended halfway all the way over to Wightman Street on the right, and then quickly dropped off on the left. There were paths everywhere, and if they didn't have plants growing, we walked on it. In some cases, we didn't care if it did, we walked and made more.

    The top of this little hill was a great place to start our BMX runs when the craze struck the neighborhood in the 1980's. Sweaty afternoons were spent digging bunny hops and table tops out of the sand pathways so we could launch our bikes from them. With the invincibility of teenagers, we never thought for a second that we could accidentally launch our bikes off the steep hillside into the pond. If someone had, we would've made fun of them for years afterwards. Like all men in training, blood was cool, someone messing up and getting hurt was funny, and if it was a serious injury, it was funny afterwards and a mark of glory for the victim. Personally, I once launched my cheap ass Huffy off a jump and came so close to hitting the tree with my brain, that I bent my right handlebar back. Like I've said, natural selection was kind where I lived.

    As soon as you walked 20 feet up the path to the top of the hill, it opened a vista that I see often in my memories. Though the land has since changed for the worse, the image will always remain with me, until I'm lying on my deathbed muttering about things no one understands. When I dream of Coggers, I always see this and when friends and I talk about it, this is what I picture.

From the hilltop, the pond spread out before you, about 20 or 30 feet below. Imagine a large gently rolling forested area, a couple miles on each side, and then scooping out all the trees and earth to a depth of 60 feet or so in search of sand. That was Coggers. Then striking water and it fills up the deepest part of your sand quarry. That was the pond. When you start reaching granite and bedrock elsewhere that aren't underwater, you start dumping piles of boulders and stumps and crap helter skelter and letting it grow in for 50 years. That was Coggers. Almost everywhere you walked out of the woods, the ground would be four or five feet higher, with mossy loam cliffs overhanging it and roots poking down into the sand. The pond itself, defied labeling shape. It was irregular with little bays and coves. Parts of it were pristine and beautiful, other areas you could see tires floating and bottles bobbing in the water. The container of choice in those days was Styrofoam and it was almost always visible somewhere when you looked. Rocks poked up here and there, sometimes with slimes of moss clinging to their sides, the tops clean, or poop covered from visiting birds. Long tall reeds of purple lustrife stood up everywhere along the water's edge and the heavy brown heads of the rushes bobbed in the wind. Looking at the water's surface, bass jumped and you'd see the rings of ripples as bluegills stupidly popped at everything that landed on the surface. At night, bats flittered, squeaking and chirping, always making you look up and flinch thinking they were going to land in your hair and give you rabies by osmosis.

I loved it.

On the other side of the pond from my street, the land was level with the water and the gravel company had dumped asphalt along the water's edge. As a kid, I remember climbing around the chunks of asphalt and fishing on it. Like everything and everywhere down there, eventually Mother Nature grew and took it over. You could still barely see the old roads the gravel company had through the woods, and the piles of crap they dumped alongside them. But standing there on my hilltop, looking outward, you saw the pond below. Basically, it looked like nature was trying to reclaim what had been disturbed, and magically, it was succeeding. It wasn't heavily forested near where I lived, but it was beginning to be. Brush poked up everywhere that we didn't tread on a daily basis, but everywhere we did, was sand. Along my edge of the pond, the gravel company was halted by the existence of houses and streets, but they still managed to dig as close as they could. Coggers near my parents' house resembled nothing more than a giant sandy bowl with the pond at the bottom.

     Looking to the right, the hillside was covered with trees and scrub brush. The white sidings of old stoves and dryers in the dump stood out among the greenery. You could see paths leading to the water's edge among the brown carpet of leaves.

     On the left side, the hillside was 30 feet above the pond, and as you followed our BMX trails around slowly, down toward the water. It gently circled around my street and the neighboring Cashin Street like a crescent, and you saw the hill drop off slowly till it was level with an area we called, "the beach." The beach was the most distant part of the pond, which you could see from where I usually stood. Its golden yellow sand stood out clearly from the vegetation around it. I was led to believe the gravel company hit water and created the pond.

I cannot express the joy I felt when I came across this one day at the library. This is how the pond looked in the 1950's.

    According to local legend, people would have picnics down there, and swim all day. One day, a child drowned, and in fear of more children drowning, and in the spirit of the 1950's, the people in the neighborhood polluted the water to keep kids from swimming there. They started the dump. They poured oil in the water and did all the good things humans can do to ruin nature. By the time I was a kid, not only was the land recovering from the gravel company's destruction, the water was as well, and it was only moderately stinky.

Overall, Coggers was a rough triangle in shape. Drum Hill Road was the left side, Route 4 the right, and Princeton Boulevard was the bottom. The gravel company was in the middle of the left side and my street was almost smack dab in the middle of the bottom. It was awesome. As a young kid, we built forts, played army, explored and started fires everyday down there, even in the middle of the summer. Matches were a premium play toy and I was always filching them from my step-dad. To this day, given a dry book of matches, I can start a fire in almost any weather. Surprisingly, given my pyromania, I only caught the woods on fire a few times. I remember one sweaty summer afternoon running up breathless to the closest adult near the woods. Sweaty and smelling like smoke we yelled, "Mr. McTeague, the woods are on fire down there!"

"Which side of the path, the upper or the lower?" he asked.

"The lower trail, call the fire department!" I replied, thinking of burning the Training School down and how I would explain it to my parents.

"Aahh let it burn out, it will do the woods good."

And that was it, we let it burn out and in a year, the woods had grown back. I loved fire as a kid, hell, given the choice of hanging indoors, doing chores all day, or lighting fires, well I lit fires. Really, how much effort goes into a fire? You sit around and throw wood on I, that's all there is to it. I loved burning things and wheat was my favorite. There were these little clusters of winter wheat that sprouted up everywhere and one good match flicked from the back of the book could ignite them, in a smooth cool motion that I excelled at. I don't know how many times I walked along setting these on fire, as my friends scrambled to put them out. In fact, that's how I set the lower woods on fire that day. When we, (read I) raked our yard, my stepfather would have me haul the leaves down to Coggers. Sensibly, it would always be the same spot so as not to cover the place with debris. He routinely ignored my suggestions and made me haul them INTO the woods, instead of the closest point to our house. Once a year, during the night, he would come up to me and say, "There's a gallon of gas in the back of my truck, take my lighter, and go down and set the leaf piles on fire." And I would get to indulge in my pyromaniac fantasies and sneak down there like a ninja, set fires, and run like hell. I loved it. The piles would burn and eventually the fire department would show up and put everything out and the leaf piles were under control for another year. Ha-ha, how different is that from now?

Like I said, back then, I was a pyro.

But it wasn't just fires that made the woods fun; it seems like every day I would go fishing. Coggers had recovered from the destruction inflicted on it by the gravel company when I was a child. In the pond there were some large bass that would taunt us with their very existence. Whole tackle boxes of lures were cast at them without as much as a glance in their direction. Allowances were spent on purchasing every lure available, all in the vain hope of landing one of these monsters. We used everything we could think of. Even going so far as to listen to hours upon hours of boring stories from our elders in the hope that they possessed some secret we lacked.

They didn't. They too had seen them, tried to catch them and failed.

We used to have legendary fishing contests among my friends, which I never ever won. Everyone would bet $5 and whoever caught the most bass in a summer would take home the purse. The right lure was the key and it could make or break a season. One year, my best friend mailed away for some Swiss Swings. They were these stupid little flashy spinners with rubber fish behind it. (Dammit, I'm not bitter.) Every stinking day we fished he would catch four bass to my one, all the while cackling madly, which drove me slowly insane as the summer progressed. One day as I cast over and over again and caught nothing, I got sick of his, "oh look, another bass," and my personal favorite, "I know you wish you had some!" statements. I looked at him with all the seriousness my 12-year-old face could muster and I swore to God that I didn't want one, ever.

A word about swearing to God, in my neighborhood, it really was the last resort of an honesty check. We grew up with great faith and if you lied after saying, "I swear to God it's true," well, we would miss ya, but you lied sucker, enjoy your time in Hell.

So three months after him getting the lures and thousands and thousands of times of responding, "Nope, I'm not telling you where I got them," and "No, you can't have one, I only have five." I swear to my creator that I don't want one of his stupid amazing Swiss Swings. He stops casting, looks at me with a stupid grin on his face and offers me one. After months of saying, "No," he is willing to speed my soul along it's (some would argue natural) course. Holding one out to me.

What a good friend.

Anytime a gaggle of kids was around and bored of playing catch, someone would say, "Let's go down cogs!" and off we would go in search of amusement. We would grab sticks to swing at everything and pull branches back to snap at those following, exploring all day long. When someone found something interesting, we would be down there the next day, with another gang of friends showing them as well. It was us who naturally kept those paths clear with our constant traipsing feet and rocks that we threw at everything. Even thedensest ofwoods weren't immune to our missions of exploration and we would just hold back branches, climb in and explore

I freely admit we were total hooligans then. I remember grabbing rocks, throwing them at the bullfrog eggs wrapped in grapelike clusters that surrounded submerged branches. "Let's see how many we can kill!" When it got close to the Fourth of July, one of our neighbors would get bricks of firecrackers and sell them to us. We would go down there and see how many things we could wreck or throw them at each other (always testing the wicks first). "Hey, let's put one in a bottle and see if it explodes…. Wheeeee!" The thought of flying shards of glass never crossed our minds. I remember my friend lighting a firecracker and he accidentally caught the rest of the pack. He threw it on the ground and stepped on it, hoping not to waste his 25 cents in one shot. He then ran screaming down the path with a pack of firecrackers glued to his foot, going off. I laughed, called him a moron and then went back to putting a firecracker in a glass beer bottle.

When I was about 11 or 12, I was lucky enough to befriend the most amazing kid. He was playing basketball in Terry's court and I stopped and asked him, "Who are you?"

"I'm me," he answered, sinking another shot, "who are you?"

"I'm Norman, I bet Steve Sousa could beat you up," I replied.

My friend Steve Sousa was a year older and my benchmark for toughness in the neighborhood.

"Can you beat up Steve Sousa?" He looked at me.

"Yes, I did before," I said.

"Then you can beat me up." He stared at me.

I looked at him, I looked at the basketball in his hands and also the bulging muscles on his forearms and made one the best decisions of my life. "Yeah I can, but I would rather shoot baskets with you." I shrugged my pathetically thin shoulders and held my hands out for the ball. That began my friendship with Eric Costa, one of the most amazing natural athletes I have ever known. We would play basketball and he would spot me 20 points and he would still win in a game of 21. Like all 12 year old best friends, we did everything together and laughed to the point of tears in the process. It was Eric that came up with the idea of playing on the ice when it wasn't safe.

After Drum Hill Sand and Gravel folded, they cleared out a huge area of the woods thinking of building there. They had put a road through one of the smaller back ponds and proceeded to fill in one half of it. They quickly paved over it and built a few brick commercial offices. They obviously didn't understand the concept of, "drainage," because after about five months of work and countless trees destroyed, about three acres of cleared lot was underwater. It wasn't deep, no more than three or maybe four feet, just enough to render it useless. With morose faces we had watched the destruction of some of Coggers, while playing on and wrecking as much construction equipment as we dared. Now that the fall rains had come, the pond was virtually indistinguishable from before. A few of our old paths were underwater and the long way around didn't really appeal to us.

As fall turned into winter, my best friend made an amazing discovery. If you walked on ice that was just barely safe, you would receive a delightful adrenalin rush when it cracked underneath you. If it broke, chances were that just your foot was going to get wet, you wouldn't fall through. Moreover, we learned if the ice was safe, it could quickly be rendered unsafe by some well placed holes. Best of all, it was hilarious. Let me tell you now, with the hindsight of 30 years, it was worth every frozen toe and wet sock. I cannot count the number of times I was doubled over with belly laughs as some unlucky soul plunged a leg into three feet of ice cold water, nor the number of times I screamed as mine went through. My friendship and the ice are best summarized in one story.

     One cold Sunday morning being experts in getting wet feet by then, we had broken a trio of holes in the ice. This formed a nice triangular path that we took turns running on at full speed. With every footstep, our weight pushed more water on the surface and we listened to it crack beneath us. You couldn't slow down, because if you did, well, doom on you and your currently dry boots. I was running on this sunny Sunday morning full speed with a slightly maniacal grin of fear on my face. All of a sudden my feet slipped out from underneath me and the next thing I know, I am enjoying looking at the woods from a seated position, about three feet off the ground. When I landed, my heels, my ass and my elbows had broken through and I was stuck, literally, I was stuck in the ice and couldn't get out. Eric came over laughing and giggling and after many comments and humor, he pulled me up. Seeing how one of us at least was miserable, we called a halt to the fun and went out to breakfast. Any laughter or joy I felt was ruined by standing in line with a wet ass and him saying, "Hey, look at this kid's butt, he had an accident," to everyone we saw. Imagine it, running across ice, watching it crack and weaken below you, waiting and hoping for your friend to fall in so you can point and laugh at him. What lunacy and what great fun. This was a ritual that we did for years. Every Fall and Spring, when the ice was unsafe, my parents could count on me coming home with soaking wet boots and I could count on getting yelled at for it. Even as an adult, I look for weak ice on shallow water and revert back to being a kid and run giggling on it.

  Sometimes we would cut through the woods and just to go to McDonald's. Much to the dismay of the employees there, we would get dirty looks whenever we walked in. Hours could be spent, just warming ourselves up and consuming our food at immeasurable slow rate. On the weekend mornings, my 12 year old self found great delight in throwing pancakes at the wall covered in syrup and betting on whose would hit the floor first. To us, that McDonald's was a slice of heaven. There was a lot of potential in that building, from popping ketchup packets at each other, to hurling iron hard butter around the dining area, it was great fun. When that grew boring, we would always return to the woods, to have a fire, or to take out his snowmobile, or just to walk and chatter like all good friends do.

  As I said before, he was a natural athlete. Being so graceful, he could dance across the tops of rocks with a pole in one hand and a tackle box in the other. He would laugh as you fell into the water trying to mimic him or planted a foot in deep mud and its sucking grasp pulled off your sneaker. Personally, my favorite was the time I miscast into a dense clump of trees. He seemed to find a great delight into my difficulty and ultimately, hilarity when my line snapped. I gave up trying to retrieve it, without the use of a machete. After asking, "You sure you can't get it?" He then went in and got it for himself. I always see that grin of his as he plunked what was formerly my lure into his tackle box.

He was that good.

The first Spring after the construction brought some amazing ice floes to the pond, and as it melted, Eric discovered one big enough to hold our weight. Call to mind you will, an image. A scrawny, tall 12 year old with a bush of hair and a muscular 13 year old who was already shaving, floating around on a slab of ice in the middle of a lake in a snowy forest. What a sight we must have presented. For that whole week, we would rush home, throw our books aside and take the ice out for a spin. Sometimes it was just Eric and I; other times someone we had brought with us. One memorable afternoon, my friend Jeff was tagging along and as we slowly poled out into the pond, showing off what we had found, the ice broke in half. Amidst our laughter and screams of excitement, I couldn't help but notice that the piece that Eric and I were on was quickly sinking. Not only did I notice it, but Jeff did too, and he pointed and started doubling over with laughter. Eric jumped across a space of about eight feet to land on Jeff's side. Once there, they started to sink, and I paddled away before Eric could jump back over and get me wet. Eventually they were able to get close enough to shore for Eric to jump, and we stood together and made fun of Jeff as he floated out there in the middle of the pond for an hour or so.

Eric was my best friend and no one ever made me laugh harder or made me have more fun doing nothing since then. He was directly responsible for the single funniest incident of my life. While I type this, I am chuckling and if I were to tell it to you out loud, I would be reduced to tears, it was that awesome. As a boy, one of our gifts was the ability to make a, "snot rocket." This is where you place one finger over a nostril and blow the other as hard as you could, (tissues not having been invented yet.) Every single male in the world knows how to do this. Usually we choose not to relieve sinus pressure in this manner, except when we are in each other's company. Anyway, at the end of my street, (next to Cog's), my friend Jeff, did this. But instead of the booger clearing his nose as usual, it stayed attached, to a length of about three feet or so. For a moment we were frozen and stood there, mouths agape, as we went from the somewhat cool manly sight of a friend blowing a snot rocket, to the hysteria of a three-foot long stripe of green booger hanging from his face. It was, instantly, the funniest thing I have ever seen. Even Jeff, who was standing there, wondering how to clear this mess from his face without getting it all over himself, was reduced to that silent quaking laughter that paralyzes. I say this, because I remember him bent over and I could see the booger tremble as he giggled silently. In the midst of this, Eric took charge of the situation, walked up, grabbed Jeff by the back of his head and shook his cranium back and forth. In three seconds, that long ass booger wrapped itself around his face three times as our laughter turned to screams. I fell over on the ground crying; indeed we all were on the ground laughing hysterically. Literally, we were all laughing so hard we were powerless to even move. I was so weak I had no strength to push Cory away as he tried to wipe his face on my pants. To this day, I can still see him lying on the ground, laughing, three lines of boogers going across his eye and wrapping around his head, and me trying weakly to push him away. Luckily the thought of his snot on my pants gave me the motivation to get up and away.

    Such a great neighborhood, such great times we had growing up, but little did we know, it was the most haunted place in North America, and we were about to find out.

CHAPTER 3

    I say it was the most haunted place in America with good reason. It was haunted, it was in America and man, when shit went down, you knew it. Now, don't get me wrong, it wasn't like something happened every single day, far from it. It was sporadic. I might have had a dozen supernatural experiences over the years down there and my friend's dozens more, but when you think that we were down there virtually everyday, that really isn't that often. What made me label it that way was the intensity of the haunting. When something happened, it wasn't a creepy sense of being watched or a shadow in the corner of your eye, that was sort of par for the course. It was something that usually made us first stop what we were doing, recognize something was wrong and then run for our lives. I've spent my life reading and learning about the spirit world and nothing I've ever heard of has come close to the things that happened in Coggers.

    As I said, we were down there almost every day; it was a great fallback place.Nothing to do? Go down Coggers, "Let's go explore," or "let's play army," or have a fire, break bottles, go fishing, etc…etc, something will turn up. Like most children, we lived oblivious to everything around us. Even though I was getting creeped out nightly by the tapping around my bedroom in my parent's house, I never thought that Coggers, a placed I loved, would be haunted as well. I think I was about 11 or 12 years old or so the first time something made me realize that the woods had something wrong with them as well.

It was a hot summers mid day and I was out and about on my usual chore of trying to amuse myself. I had gone up to Drum Hill alone and since I was alone I was going to have a fire. I had gotten a cardboard box from one of the many dumpsters there, and I took it with me into the woods, making sure to walk far enough in so that no one would see the smoke. To those who have never had the experience of watching a box burn, I can tell you that it's a pretty cool thing - especially to a young, budding pyromaniac. As I said, I was trying to amuse myself

I get away from my point. On this summer's day, I had my box, I lit it and was watching it burn with anavid intensity. As it caught fire, I heard a dog barking, way off in the distance, it was enough that I acknowledged it, "hey that's a dog," and I went back to watching the box burn. That's the way I remember it, as soon as the box was lit, I heard a dog barking. I am watching the walls collapse and I continue to hear the dog, somewhat louder, barking nonstop. It burns, I watch, dog barks and this continues for a few minutes until I realize the barking is getting louder. The dog is getting closer and closer and to be honest, it doesn't sound like a little terrier or a little wiener dog. This is a big dog, like a German shepherd or something larger and it sounds like it's heading right towards me and, really, it's moving fast too, like an animal at full sprint. . I picked up an old Toyota truck tailgate that was lying on the ground, threw it on the sad remnants of my box, (it was mostly gone anyway), and I stomped it out. I'm a pyro, but I don't want to burn the woods down, I might get grounded again.

So I put my fire out and start walking down the trail, thinking of how I would like to be exploring a retail establishment, as opposed to being at the woods at the moment. The paths in the top half of Coggers were in these lazy "S"shapes, they all ran parallel to each other. So as I walk, I'm listening to this dog and I realize that it's going to take about 10 minutes for me to get out of the woods. I had walked too far in! Now I am a couple hundred yards from my fire and I notice from the sound, the dog, he's veered off his original course and is heading for my new location. I don't know what point the, "holy crap I'm about a half mile from civilization and other people and there's a freaking large ass dog heading through the woods for me," but I clearly remember just picking up and running. I started heading down the path, but as I ran I knew it was going to take too long. I could hear movement through the undergrowth as this animal brushed shrubs and leaves aside. I stopped for a moment and thought to myself, "It's gonna take me 10 minutes to run out via the trails, or I can cut through and get out of here in three minutes." Since the barking was getting louder and I was as far from people as a kid with a dog after him wants to be, I ran up a small hill and down into the woods. Screw the paths.

Let me tell you something, at forty, I can outrun my children on their bikes. Then, I was a skinny little kid with no extra meat on me; I could run like the wind. I could move, and that day, I ran for my life. Imagine, a sunny summer day and there's a 12 year old kid running as fast as he can through the woods, over little rises, through stands of water with cat o' nine tails growing, jumping and leaping. All in the effort of getting away from the dog that he hears running behind him, which from the sounds of it, is severely pissed off. I can still see it clearly in my mind's eye, still remember my panting breath. Now it's getting close, and I can hear it barking and its claws scrabbling on the hardscape as it chases after me. My over riding thought was to get to Drum Hill, where people were.

"Hey lady, look at that dog mauling that kid, let's go help him."

I don't know why, but as I burst from the brush and came out onto one of the many paths back behind the stores there, I headed for the Burger King. Even at 12, I was street smart and coming up behind a strip mall to their back doors wouldn't help me if this dog started using my leg for a chew toy. I needed people, like the kind that might be going into BK for a cheeseburger and would help a 12 year old kid from being attacked by some loud ass dog that didn't want him burning a box in the woods.

As I started running up towards Burger King, (Remember, that almost all of Drum Hill was about eight or so feet higher than Coggers), I realized two things. One, this thing was right behind me, I could hear its panting breath, it was going nuts and before I got much farther, it was going to grab a leg of mine and start shaking. The second was that I could run to the top of this path and get a swing in before it grabbed me. I might have an advantage being higher, or that I could continue to run and it was going to take me down. Either way, my already belligerent nature had decided that if something was about to bite me, I was going to try and punch it first. As I ran up the hill and got to the top, I turned with my fist cocked ready to fight for my life.

There was nothing there.

Nothing.

No more barking, no dog, just some grubby, skinny kid who smelled like smoke and was standing there on the top of a small rise, panting with his fist cocked.

I started crying.

Yeah, I cried, wouldn't you? What the hell? There was no way I dreamt that. I was breathing hard and adrenalin was coursing through my veins. I looked around for the dog, thinking that it had slunk off, but it wasn't there; there was nothing, just rocks and trees. I looked at my pant legs and sneakers again, they were wet, from my dash through the woods. I slowly uncocked my fist. Let me tell you something, it messed with my head. I looked around a few more times, now hoping to see it. I wiped my eyes and I slowly walked down Drum Hill Road and down Princeton Boulevard toward home. I remember telling my friends at the time about it and them agreeing and saying "wow man." And although I was known as a liar to my parents and an exaggerator of tales to my friends, I don't think one of them doubted my story was true.

I know that your natural inclination is to doubt and think, "No, he was a little kid, it probably ran off before he got out" No, this part of the woods was wide open, if it ran off, I would have seen it when I turned around. In fact, I spun around because it was so close; I knew I was going to get bit. When I told this to Chris and Dave one night in the woods, I recorded a great EVP. **PLAY EXACTLY EVP**

I remember staying out of Coggers for a few days; no phantom dog was going to chew on me if I could avoid it. I forget what made me head back down there, probably until Eric said, "let's go fishing," and I said, "OK," knowing if I was with him, nothing would dare chase him through the woods.

Something had changed for me after that. I started being more aware of what was going on around me when I was there. Before, all I had to worry about was the tough kids from the low income housing near Drum Hill. (Occasionally, they would tire of beating people up there and come down Coggers to look for fresh game). Now, I kept one part of my mind attuned to the woods themselves, in case I heard that dog again. Instead of breaking bottles all day there, if I felt spooky, I left.

Even being home was no respite from the place. Since my parents lived on a street that, "DEAD ENDED," (insert creepy music here) into Coggers, in the Spring and Summer, with my windows open, I started noticing I always heard odd things at night now. Sometimes it would be animals screaming down there, other times people talking and a few times, human screams. Oh joy, no better chamber music to fall asleep to than distant screaming. I don't remember how many nights I lay in bed, listening to the woods with just my eyes poking above the blanket. Once in a while I would hear something that defied logic and I would pull my covers over my head and try to fall asleep. Other times it would be the local teenagers drinking beer and laughing. Beyond the simple noises, the time with the dog changed the woods for me in more ways than I can explain. I wasn't alone either. As my youth turned me into an obnoxious teenager, more and more of my friends told me stories of their own. It was like our age protected us, it was a natural immunity, and only as we became older, with our own personalities, did Coggers make itself known to us.

I can recall a few times walking through the woods at night with Eric, hearing footsteps behind us, or with other friends, (which will be covered in another chapter), but after the dog, nothing scary happened to me for awhile. It was like once the woods had spent itself it went dormant and rested. I learned to listen to my instincts far more often. If I was down there and felt odd, or if it felt like something was watching me, I would wrap up what I was doing and head out. Even walking in, if the woods didn't feel right, I would turn around and do something else. Never with friends, I was always brave in the company of others. I think it came from knowing I could outrun most of them, so if something happened, they would die, not me. From then on though, if I was alone and felt weird, I would change my plans. Aside from the screaming woman of the summer nights, it was pretty quiet (more on her later).

When I was 17, I had a girlfriend named Katrina. She was a lovely young lady, with a great smile and glasses, who didn't seem to mind that I was thin or had a giant bush of hair. I wore glasses too, but only to school since I thought I looked like a total dork in them.

One night in late May we were out together with a co-worker of ours (His car, neither of us had one back then), when upon our mutual agreement we decided we wanted to fool around. Now, by then I had a place in the pine forest near Route 4 where I would take willing girlfriends who I wore down with constant whiny pestering. Since we were only 17 at the time, hotel rooms and bedrooms were ruled out by parents and limited funds, so we improvised. My spot was ideal; some daytime scouting had located an almost perfect circle of baby pines about four feet high, in among the older ones of the forest. This area of Coggers had pine trees planted with almost German precision. It enabled someone to alternately look through the whole forest and not see beyond 10 feet of the nearest tree trunk. An old car trail ran alongside it parallel to Route 4. The forest itself started level with Technology Drive and the trail, and then gently rose to point of about four or five feet above it. It was shaped like a long drawn out triangle with the trail on one side and open rocky areaon the other, it tapered as it approached Drum Hill Road. Since Technology Drive was just being put in, it was paved but not lighted, so we had my friend Rich drop us off along the side of the forest from there. As we left the safety of his giant car, he looked around and asked, "Are you sure you guys want to be dropped off here?"Even Katrina looked like she was having second thoughts; it was a pitch black night with no moon, and a bit windy out. But when I grabbed her hand and looked her in the eyes, she agreed and hormones prevailed, well someone's hormones anyway.

  We started walking in, it wasn't far, maybe a couple hundred feet from where we were dropped off. I had blankets stashed there and we started making it comfortable for us. I wasn't a boy scout as a kid, but I lived by some of the principles. Katrina and I had been here on my birthday back in March and a few times since, (Don't ask about the blankets ok? They were protected from the elements.) So she knew the place as well. We made it as comfortable as blankets in a pine forest can be on a May night. As I recall it now, I remember I was kind of freaked out. It just didn't feel right, there was something odd and off about that night. It was something that I should've recognized immediately given all my experiences I had, had there already, but as I said " Hormones ruled." The whole time we were there, being intimate, I kept thinking of the, "Friday the 13th," where Jason spears the couple together through the bed.

  Really, I am laying there making out with this hot young lady and thinking of being speared to the ground. Not really what I had in mind when I convinced her to go with me. All of a sudden I become aware of an odd noise, it was so amiss that it took my attention from those soft lips and made both of us pause and listen for a few seconds. We stoppedand since it didn't sound evil or like a dog running through the woods at me, I grabbed her and we went back to what we were doing.

The next day when we talked about it, she said, to her, it sounded like demonic laughter. To me, it sounded like a helicopter landing between two walls, a reverberating noise. That's the closest description I can come to after 25 years of time passing. I distinctly remember telling my friends about it and saying it sounded like that. I know you're wondering how two people can hear two completely different things, (continue on and I will explain later) suffice to say, we did. **PLAY HEY CAT EVP**

So we hear this noise, I sit up, look around, I don't see Jason running at me with a spear like I had been imagining, and I don't hear anything else, especially not a barking dog, so I get back to work.

Hormones ruled the day.

Afterwards, we were lying there talking, (pine needle talk I guess it would've been called), laying there and enjoying the bond that love creates, just relaxing and hugging each other when we heard a knocking noise. KNOCK! That's exactly what it sounded like, a loud hard knock, and then I heard another and another and another.

Yeah, I know, as I read this, I realize how lame it sounds....whoopee a knocking noise, but remember, this was Coggers, and I knew every sound every animal made in those woods. I knew what people sounded like moving through the brush, plus, IT WAS COGGERS, and you always paid attention when down there at night, or at least AFTER sex you did. I knew those woods like the back of my hand and here was something new. So I stood up on shaky legs and looked around, peering into the dark to try and see something. Whatever it was, it was coming from the area of Drum Hill Road and I was staring above the little pines in that direction when I heard it again. Another knock and then another, it sounded like someone was taking a big branch and just whacking a tree with it, as hard as they could. (I've since simulated this noise by doing exactly that. Try it, it's fun). As I looked deeper into the pines from where I thought the sound was coming from, my brain processed that the sound was moving. It wasn't someone just standing there whacking a tree trunk as hard as they could, it was shifting all over the compass. Think of a clock, if I'm at six o'clock, I hear the noise at one o'clock, and then 11 o'clock, and then two o'clock, you get the idea.

I'm crouching behind these trees and hearing this noise moving and Katrina asks, "What is it?" It's getting louder and louder which means it's getting closer. Now as I peer over these tree tops, I see movement on the old car trail. Without my glasses, my vision sucks, but I can make out something white in the trail. As I watch it, I hear the knocking noise again and it jumps, yes jumps, because that's the only way to describe how something moves 20 feet in the space of a second. I watch it for three seconds and hear, "knock, knock, knock," and this thing has covered 60 feet of trail. And size? It was much bigger than a bird and smaller than a moose, since it's on the car trail, it's four or five feet below the ground I am on, and I can still see it.

I see it clearly in my mind's eye, how it looked to me that night, a white blurry shape, jumping down the trail and out of my line of sight, and I remember how I felt then. As I sit here typing this, in broad daylight, I am hit with the energy of it again, and I get the chills.

Fuck me, I am staring at where I saw it last and thinking fast. I looked at Katrina and said, "Get your fucking clothes on, we're getting out of here."The first thing I do is crouch down and feel around for a weapon. My hand comes across a good size stick with some heft. I am sure the Irish would have called it a shillelagh. As Katrina dresses, I am pulling on my clothes as fast as I can one handed while staring into the forest, my brain working feverishly. I finish and I'm standing there with adrenalin pumping through my veins, handing her, her things, coat, gloves, trying to speed up this process, because we need to move, and NOW. That is the overriding feeling, GET OUT, get out fast and get out alive. When I hand her, her belt, I feel the size of it and since it was the 1980's, it weighed about 10 pounds and it feels like it could crush someone's skull like an egg. I tell her, "ifanything comes out of the woods at us, just start swinging this and don't stop."She looks at me with wide eyes and goes to ask a question but I am already taking her hand and leading her away.

I use all my skill and knowledge to get us out of the woods as quickly and quietly as possible. That walk out of the woods, with me leading, was pretty damn scary, even if it was only a few hundred feet. It was pitch black and even though I can move in the forest at night like a cat, I hadn't heard that knocking sound for awhile now. This meant it was either far away or worse, waiting somewhere close and watching, getting ready to chew on us in a painful manner.

As we walked out onto the road without incident, I breathed a sigh of relief and we started heading up Technology Drive toward Drum Hill Road. Now I have two choices; I can walk 200 feet back toward Route 4 and the darkened houses that line that road, or I can walk a couple of thousand feet toward Drum Hill Road and life. Personally, I had seen too many horror movies to walk towards darkened houses, which was also closer to the car trail where I had seen whatever the fuck it was bouncing along. So we started walking down Technology Drive, on guard, but a bit more relaxed since we were out of the woods and in the relative open but that passed quickly. You see, they were putting the sewerage in at the time, so there were these huge concrete cylinders lining the roads. Pipes, culverts, the junctions where they all meet, you get the idea. As we walked along, hand and hand, my eyes were rolling every which way, trying to take it all in, trying not to be surprised by anything.I will always remember that walk down the road in the dark. No moon and the cylinders stacked on either side of us, just dark shapes, preventing me from seeing anything clearly, I was constantly looking up at them, with adrenalin pumping through my veins. To me, that was the scariest part, because a whole horde of winged monkeys could've jumped down from them and carried us off to the wicked witch, or whatever it was out there. It could've jumped us in a second, and we wouldn't have been able to do anything about it. Well, except take a swing at them with the belt and a stick.

    Eventually we cleared that part of the construction site and were just walking along the road and more familiar open territory. As we approached a fenced in area that protected a construction trailer for the site, (fenced in to protect it from my friends and I), I was just about to breathe a sigh of relief when we heard a noise. To this day this is all I can say, "I heard a noise." But it wasn't anything like a duck or a knocking noise. This was a cascading sound, like a series of loud metal dominos falling over, each making a sound. It literally made the hair stand up on the back of my neck. I looked at Katrina and asked, "Did you hear that?"

    "Yes."

"Do you know what that is?"

"No."

"Are you scared?"

"Wicked."

I looked at her and with all the self-assuredness of my 17 year old, 140 pound frame could muster and said, "If anything happens, I want you to run as fast as you can toward Drum Hill." She asked me what I was going to do, but I had decided as I had a few times before, if anything was going to happen, I was going down swinging. I wasn't letting this woman, who I loved, get hurt. We started along again, even more aware, quieter and nothing happened. We walked down Technology Drive and reached Drum Hill not talking, both just focused on listening, (damn right we weren't taking the shorter path through the woods), and then down Princeton Boulevard to my street and to my parents' house.

We went upstairs to my room and were sitting in my bed, silent, in a daze or at least a mild state of shock. I can't speak for her, but I know I was. We were just sitting there on my bed holding each other, relieved to be alive, when we heard it screaming. We are laying there hugging and I hear whatever it is calling from Coggers. It is was running along the path from Wightman Street to Corey and back, calling the whole time. To me, it sounded like a dog and owl mixed together, like a repetitive bark…ar… ar… ar… ar… We looked at each other and realized we hadn't gotten away after all, it had let us go. It felt like it knew we were there, listening and it just wanted to say, "Hiya, miss me yet?" To me, it sounded like it was mocking me, calling out, saying, "Ha-ha, I'm still here moron." I felt crappy all over again, and whatever sense of relief we had evaporated.

I walked her home that night. The next day I happened to catch my neighbor in the street. "Did you hear some animal last night down Coggers?" I asked her. When she said she did, and in return asked me, "What the hell was it?" I knew she had no clue either but I felt a little better because it wasn't just us.

That screwed me up. Unlike the phantom dog, this was tangible; I had seen it and had a witness with me. I went to school the next day and confided to all my friends. Whether it was my seriousness or they were humoring me, a few days later we were down there at night with bats and knives. Needless to say, we didn't find anything. I am glad, because 20 or so teenagers, walking through Coggers with samurai swords and butterfly knives, are dangerous and stupid.

Things picked up after that. I don't mean that the next day something creepy happened, but it wasn't long after I got the crap scared out of me again.

One summer night I was laying in bed reading Stephen King's, great book, "It." It was late, and everyone was asleep in the house. The way my bedroom was set up, (indeed my parents' house, the layout itself was a bit odd), was when you walked through the gate into the backyard and our main entrance, you walked below an open roofed structure. This was great in the summer; it had chairs under it and ran the length of the house, stopping only when it reached the door. My bedroom faced this roof on one side and the street on the other. During the summer, I would move my bed so that my head rested behind the window that opened out on to the roof. Sometimes I could catch a cool breeze. When I say sometimes, I mean never, so I can't really explain why I did this, I just did. So this night, as I lay in my bed sweating, reading, "It," I got the feeling of being watched. Now being watched was nothing new in my parents' house, since it was as haunted as the woods next to it, but as I lay there, I stopped reading because I started hearing breathing. Not your normal breathing either, this sounded heavy, like someone with emphysema masturbating. I put down my book and looked out the window into the blackness, and I couldn't see anything. The breathing got louder. This sounded like some kind of bad joke, whatever it was, it was panting and breathing really heavy, and as I type this, I get the goose bumps again. I looked at the window and said, "Fuck you," flipped it the bird and ran down into my parents' bedroom.

"Wake up, something's on the roof!"

"Hrmmm," came the sleepy reply.

"Mom and dad wake up, there is something on the roof!"

My step-dad actually sprang to his feet when I said this and looked at me and said, "What's up, what's going on?"

"Dad, I am 19 years old, I'm not a little kid and I don't get scared easy, there is something on the roof."

Even my mom had woke up at this point, and as we stood there in the dark in my parents' bedroom, we all heard a thump as something landed from the roof to the lawn. I stared at them as if to say, "see," and we hear it hit the chain link fence that surrounds the yard.

We look at each other in the dark and my step-dad said, "Whatever it is, it's gone now, go back to bed."

That ended that conversation, no, let's call the cops, or let's go check it out, just, go back to bed. For awhile afterwards I was asking myself, "Was it someone beating off to me reading IT?" But a few years later my brother told me his story, along the exact same lines, except in his version he went to my old room and stuck a knife out and then looked outside, there was nothing there.

Also, so many times in Coggers, the spirits there physically interacted with the world. Once they became dense enough to be heard, they were dense enough to affect the world and therefore jump on the ground. That's my story and I'm sticking to it.

Great, so not only do I now have to worry about when down in the woods, or listening to the spirit world tapping in my bedroom wall/bookcase/stereo, I have to think about what could potentially happen while lying in bed. This is what I mean when I say it picked up. Stuff started happening every year, and when I would tell the friends I ran into in the neighborhood, they would nod and shake their heads, and we would say, "Coggers," together and look towards the woods.

When I was in my late teens, and starting to party every night, I began to show brief episodes of higher thinking. With a stepfather who had a penchant for violence and a 4 a.m. wake up time, I was smart enough not to take any chances with a carload of loud idiots dropping me off. Instead of stopping in front of my house, making noise and doing a 40 point turn out, they left me at the bottom of Cashin Street and drove away. I would take the path through the woods home. After what happened to Katrina and me, I started listening and paying attention as I walked that path. I mean, think about it, with just a phantom dog here, a masturbating ghost there, I had went from oblivious to alert. Even walking a few hundred well known feet through the woods at night alone had become spooky as hell to me.

I listened when I was in the woods. I guess some of the innocence was already going. A few times I had heard animal movement through the leaves near me and one night I heard something real big over by Wightman Street. It sounded like a bear was rolling around in the leaves over there. I kept my focus and attention on it and headed quickly, (and quietly), home. About a month later as I made my way down the path, I was so drunk that as I walked, all I could think was, "I'm so fucked up, I'm so fucked up," over and over again. About 100 feet from the end of the trail, I stopped all of a sudden because I realized that in my fugue, I hadn't even listened. I remember very clearly, that being my thought, "shit I haven't even listened yet!" The moment I thought that, I heard a loud thump in the path right behind me. Picture the noise someone would make, jumping out of the lower branches of a tree and landing flat feet on the ground that was the noise!

RIGHT BEHIND ME!

I don't even remember running. I just found myself slowing to a stop in my parents' driveway and putting my hand on the back of my neck to feel the hair standing on end. If you've never had the hair stand on the back of your neck, let me tell you, it's a very unpleasant experience. I looked at the woods and said, "fuck you," and went in with a whimper. From then on, I had my friend's drop me off at the top of the street and I walked down. Screw Cashin Street and the woods, I wasn't going through that again. A great part to this story is that 20 years later, I was in the woods and I was standing next to the very tree that this had happened under and I was telling this story, we got a very clear "bleah". **PLAY BLEAH EVP**

When I was 20 years old, my parents took my younger brothers to the beach for the weekend, leaving me the house. I was pretty excited, here I was 20, it was a Friday night and while I didn't have any parties planned, (I wasn't stupid; just occasionally retarded, my dad would've destroyed me), I did have some company coming over the next night. But more importantly and harder to communicate, was the fact that I didn't have to answer to anyone but myself or behave. And if I wanted to walk around nude or sit in the TV room eating Doritos, no problemo.

It was a hot June evening and I remember running through the house and opening every window. It was so nice out, the kind of early summer night that makes all the snow and rain worthwhile in New England. I was sitting in our TV room, just feeling the breeze blowing in as the sun set, when I heard this man screaming for help. Not yelling, "Hey help me here," but full on screaming at the top of his lungs. It was just how someone being tortured would sound. Seriously, it went from me watching TV to turning down the volume to listen to a man scream for his life. It was faint, off in the distance, but audible, which made me think its location was either in the back of the Training School, or the hill and party spot. Either way, it was pretty far off, but clear. It went something like this, "Please, please no! God no! Please help me, aggghhhhh, please don't please. Nooooooo, agh, please don't dooonnn't!" Honestly, that's what I heard. Since this was Coggers, I went and closed every window in the house turned on the AC and got my brother's baseball bat and a large kitchen knife and put them in the room with me. I fell asleep fitfully and with one eye open. And while I did enjoy my weekend alone, that kind of put a damper on my excitement.

When my parents returned, my dad found the knife in the TV room, held it out to show it to me, and said, "Pussy." I didn't bother explaining. Why? He wouldn't believe me, and would probably think I was nuts, and more importantly, he might not have let me stay alone again.

When I told this story as an adult to a friend and they asked me, "Did you call the cops?" and "Why not?" when I told them I didn't, that this was Coggers and stuff like this happened. If someone was being murdered down there, well it wouldn't be the first time as far as I could tell and it wouldn't be the last. But more importantly and what makes me wonder, is the thought never even crossed my mind.

In my early 20's I went down to the woods one night with a friend of mine to split a six pack of beer and talk about old times. He and I walked down the paths till we came to the remnants of the beach area. There, we drank our beers and talked and laughed for awhile. As was my wont back then, I asked him if he believed in ghosts, when he replied no, I proceeded to tell him about some of the things that had happened to my friends and I over the years. When I got done, he said, "well Norman, I don't think you're a liar, I just don't think it happened the way you remembered it."

That was pretty kind and I accepted it for what it was, we had finished our beers and agreed it was time to leave. As we walked up the upper path, with him in front of me, we noticed the leaves on the ground alongside us rustling. As if the wind was blowing in a hard, steady manner, the only thing was, it wasn't. He noticed it first and stopped dead in his tracks, slowly saying "what the ???" I stopped as well and looked around, it seemed that around us in a large circle of say, seven or eight feet on either side of the path the leaves were rustling. I looked about, I heard a ticking noise, like something was hitting branches, and sure enough, I saw individual branches on bushings twitching as I heard this tick, tick tick. Almost as if something invisible was hitting them. He looked at me and asked, "What the hell is this?"

I smiled and said, "You want to see something cool Brian?"I walked toward him, well, as I did, the rustling leaves moved forward with me and as I walked back away, they followed me back.

"I'm getting the fuck out of here!" He shouted as he ran up the path and out of the woods. I ran after him laughing, asking if he still didn't believe in ghosts. Ha-ha

These are a few of the big things. I don't mention the hundreds of times I was dropped off and I stood in my driveway, staring at my parents' dark yard with foreboding. Feeling like something was there, just behind the gate, on the right, watching me, waiting for me to walk back there so it could eat me. Sometimes I would go to my stepfather's truck and grab something heavy to swing in case I was attacked. I would walk through the gate and assume an attack posture, and then place it on the steps as I made my way into the house. Lord did that piss my step-dad off, when he went looking for the tool the next day on the job. Other times I would just take my chances and run back there. So many times, so many times I was scared. I would walk in through the gate, look to my right in the hidden corner, with a fist raised, and then walk into the house. Then I'd get upstairs and lie there, and listen to the spirits in my room tapping, or the Coggers creature screaming down in the woods. I also didn't mention the screaming woman who made a regular yearly appearance when I turned 12, but aside from all things I had experienced, I had one thing going for me,

At least I wasn't alone.

CHAPTER 4

I have stories up the wazoo about the woods and I've skipped a bunch of them. I wasn't alone in the weird and Coggers combination department. A lot of my childhood friends had tales that defied explanation, not all of them, but enough to make me feel better when I realized it just wasn't me and an odd combination of chemicals in my brain. That was something that reassured me over the years, because there were times when I asked, "Is it me? Am I completely insane?" Some of my closer friends knew when I got a certain look in my eye, that I would start talking about Coggers and the supposed monster that I thought lived there. After Katrina and I, I thought it was an animal of some sort, something tangible. As I remember it, I was never called an out and out liar, which was represented in my area by, "You're full of shit." Other times peoples' eyebrows would rise and sometimes I would get a mere, "Weird," and a quick change of conversation. While you might think, "if it was so haunted and you ran for your life crying like a baby, how come you kept going down there?"

Understand that Coggers was a magical place, one where I fished, built fires, played all day, hiked, and explored. It's cut-through saved about 20 minutes on the walk to Drum Hill. When something strange happened, or something haunted, I might stay away for a week, but then one of my friends would want to go down there. Or I would forget, and then when I was down there remember. More importantly, since I didn't want to be labeled the ultimate term of shame in my neighborhood, "a pussy," I would go. A lot of the kids in the old neighborhood had stories too. They usually came up in conversation when one of us would say, "Let's go down Cogs and break bottles" or "let's go start a fire, "and then they wouldn't want to (and weren't afraid of being called a pussy), and then would tell us how something had happened. We would talk about it and share stories, freak each other out, and in the end, just chalk it up to, "Well that's Coggers." That was the thing, you just never knew. Sometimes things happened, mostly they didn't.

While I might have had five or ten paranormal experiences that happened to me over the years, there were friends out there who had an equal amount, if not more. Then there were the lucky few who never had anything happen to them at all. It was odd and a little bit intriguing how I could be chased from the woods by a phantom dog, run panting and crying, swearing that I'd never to go down to Coggers again. Then talk to someone the next day who looked at me like I was speaking Aramaic when I told them why I didn't want to go there.

Over the years I've bent some thought to it, and there was one thing all of us weirdo's had in common, we all grew up in dysfunctional families. All those that had supernatural Cogger's experiences, had hard childhoods. I'm not sitting here and laying the blame for anything on anyone, nor am I trying to add to an already long list of my parents' crimes, but I know that growing up with an alcoholic stepfather, I was always intensely aware of the emotion in the house. I could walk in and sense exactly the mood of the place, whether I could watch TV or should just run up to my room and try to avoid doom. My other friends with stories had families similar to mine, in some cases worse. Those, with what we would consider normal families, had very few incidents of the paranormal, indeed, almost none. While I am not saying their childhoods weren't difficult, they didn't have to be aware all the time of what left their mouths for the fear of a back hand. It's interesting because you can find this in almost every famous medium of the supernatural.

Inevitably, when I talk to someone about the spirit world and they've had experiences, I will always ask, "Your family was dysfunctional, eh?" They agree and then I explain my theory. It's like that suffering either opens you up to it or makes you hyperaware of your surroundings. While sharing painful memories wasn't something that was done in my era, I know and knew that some of my friends had hard childhoods. When you knocked on someone's door and they couldn't come out, you could assume they got the shit kicked out of them for something we had done the day before. And when someone always has to have one eye open for what was going on in their supposed place of safety, you tend to be more aware of things then the average person. It's either that or they are just empathetic people, those that can feel emotion, attract spirits. In fact, the recent trend I've seen among psychics is to say that to everyone, "Oh you must be very empathetic."

So someone is either hyperaware of emotion or empathetic and sensitive and that attracts the spirit world. And I will bet the last 50 cents in my pocket, that if you're reading this and have had a lot of experience with ghosts, that you are one of these things. Ultimately at your most basic sense, according to science, you are energy. All matter is a form of energy, shaped and transformed into molecules and atoms but energy all the same. More importantly we all have these energy fields around us. **All of us, whether you are aware of it or not.**

I refuse to go into this in great detail, because many far better authors have done a far better job than I ever will. But basically, everything you think, know, believe, shows up in your energy field. Every second of the day, every thought process you have, influences your energy field. Guess what, if you believe in ghosts, you are more likely to have something supernatural happen to you than someone who doesn't.

Duh Norman!

Good people, attract good things. Bad people, well, watch the news to see what bad people attract. Since this energy field surrounds you every moment of the day and everything you feel is a form of energy, it shows up. Ever notice how you get a chill AFTER you think something? It's your energy field resetting itself to show your new belief.

Let me take credit for that, and read it again. When you feel a chill, it will be after you convince or think of something new. It's your energy field resetting itself.

Now, since a spirit is pure energy, they see it, and they can see when someone is empathetic or sensitive. Since those are just ways of being open to emotions and hence in your energy field, the spirit world sees that and clamors for your attention. Think about it, since the only way a spirit can make itself known to you is to project emotion or energy - which is emotion at its most basic form - wouldn't you look for people who could sense emotion? Of course you would. If I am an angry spirit, or a sad one, who will know I am around? Someone who is sensitive to energy, whatever was down Coggers, really projected emotion and those of us sensitive to it, well, we felt it. This is a collection of those stories, gathered up from my friends, as adults, by me.

    Through the power of harassing emails, phone calls and my basic ability of being a jerk and not quitting at stuff, I managed to get in touch with about half of my childhood friends. A lot of the people I wanted to talk to, I haven't been able to find even with the magic of Facebook. Life goes on, they've moved on, and their parents have moved as well. There was one childhood friend in particular that was with me a few times when we ran out of the woods. She was with me and Steve Sousa when we heard that thing calling for us that you will read about. I had really wanted to talk to her. When I stopped by her parents' house and asked after her, her dad told me, "nah she lives in Florida, now." I guess since she had moved, she no longer existed to him. I thank God my parents didn't disown me when I moved out of state. From the way he has always acted around me and from the way he acted then, (also from all the mischief her and I got into as kids!) I can deduce that she was like me, someone with a crappy hard family, hence the reason so many things happened down Coggers when we were together. Hopefully she's made her way in the world and has found peace within herself like I finally did.

    Tom Guertin was a friend who moved to the neighborhood when I was about 11 or 12. He was a year younger than I. With bright red hair and a stocky (I won't call him fat) body, he and I made friends pretty quickly. He and a friend of mine were the first to hear the screaming woman (among my friends anyway). I heard it a couple of times too, growing up and I don't exactly remember when in the hazy memory of childhood, but I do remember the shrieks very well. But when he and Kevin heard it, well, let him tell the story.

Tom:

"The first thing I remember is, we were by the chain link fence by the bike track where you could get across (the path that ran between Corey street and Wightman Street) and Kevin and I heard a woman scream for help and we had the police there and there was nothing."

Basically, he and Kevin were walking down the path near my house and they heard the woman calling for help. They got scared, (since they were younger than I and it was just the two of them), and called the cops. The police came down, searched the area, and left, leaving these kids to wonder what they had heard.

Now, don't think for a second it was a quick, "Help!" and that's it. No, this was a woman screaming bloody murder, "heeeeeelp, someone please heeeeeelp me," over and over again. Loud, very loud, it wasn't anything you would hear and think it was something else. No, this was a woman screaming for her life.

I think, (again the memory fails me), we were about 12 when I was with my friends and I heard it for the first time, and I remember us all running into the woods, looking around, and finding nothing. Walking out confused and wondering what the hell we just heard. The following year when were playing baseball in my street, we heard it again, and we looked at each other. I think someone asked if we should go get help and the rest of us said, "No, there's nothing there." One of my childhood friends, Jimmy Woods, also confirms that story; the woman screaming, yelling for her life. When we met to talk about it, he told me, "I heard her a few times," when I mentioned it to him. I heard it a few more times too as well, as I got older. It was always the same voice, screaming the same things.

That's the thing that blows my mind about Coggers and the presences there. It was so powerful. Most hauntings are very weak and it takes a spirit tremendous amounts of energy to break through the veil into this dimension. In Coggers not only did it break through, it came through with attitude and everyone would hear it, and usually, we ran for our lives.

My younger brother Peter has the best story about the lady of Coggers. He was with a bunch of friends up in the party spot next to Brownie Hill drinking. He was about 19 years old or so and there with about 10 other teens. They had a roaring bonfire and my brother turned to his friends and asked, "Do you guys believe in ghosts? Cause this place is really haunted." They replied, "Shut the fuck up Pete, no one wants to hear that bullshit," **and**, "No."As he tells it, about five minutes later they heard the woman screaming *"way off in the distance, everyone kind of shut up and listened to it. As we listened, we realized it was getting closer, until it sounded like it was on the next path over from us. But the thing was, you couldn't hear any movement through the woods, not a branch, not leaves, nothing, just this woman screaming for help."*

I asked him, "What did you guys do?"

"We ran for our lives."

I laughed because I knew what he meant. Think about it though, here's a group of teenagers, like 15 or 20 of them, hanging out drinking beer, and they hear this. But instead of being fearless like normal teenagers, they ran.

There is something about the truly paranormal that causes unreasonable fear. Pan the Greek God was known for causing panic (hell, that's where we get the word from) and I am far from saying that Pan exists in 40 acres of woods in Chelmsford, MA, but I am pointing out that when something truly supernatural occurs, panic sets in. Countless times when something was happening, I was scared to hell. Even in the beginning of this book, when that thing came out, for about 10 seconds, I was scared.

Tom continues,

"Another time was when we had the hay fort that Ryan and Jeff,(two other youths from the neighborhood I haven't been able to contact) had built me. Kevin and I were in it and someone called Jeff's name. We got out and looked and there was no one there so we got back in and then it happened three more times and no one was around."

When I was 12, the sand and gravel pit closed. They took all the land and cleared it out, destroying a lot of it. They built commercial offices where the gravel company had been and put in a road that bisected Coggers in half and connected Route 4 and Drum Hill Road. They at least made some kind of effort at conservation, (though I will say it was very poor) in that they put hay bales up where they were supposed to prevent soil from running off into the water. Well, being deviant kids, we took them, and made big forts out of them. Hey, nothing is cooler than a two by four foot hay bale of Lego's.

So Tom and a friend are in there and they hear their names being called, no biggie, just interesting, especially three times.

Tom,

"Another time I was with Jimmy Woods and we built a little fire in a small hay fort we had, and it started to catch on fire. Some guy where the office buildings were started to scream at us, so we got scared and ran. But we did not go far, when we turned around the fire was out, but when we ran it was huge." Could be vagaries of the wind, of hay burning, could be anything, but still interesting.

"Another time I was walking back from behind Burger King. It was about 9:00 p.m. and I heard something behind me. When I looked and did not see anything, I kept walking. Then I saw the bushes move and I heard my nick name, "lumpy." But Tony Spinacha was the only one who really called me that so I ran like a bastard and I kept hearing someone behind me, but did not see anything. Well, when I got to the clearing right before party rock I stopped and I kept hearing my name, "lumpy," but there was nothing and it scared the shit out of me so bad I did not go back there until me and moose." (Moose being the nick name for the largest kid in the neighborhood, Scott Costa, brother to my best friend Eric)

That area behind Burger King was well known. I had heard laughter back there and that was where the dog chased me too. He's down there, and something is calling his name, he starts to run and it chases after him, whenever he stops, it calls his name. Do you think that it would freak you out? I can't tell you the number of stories I've gotten, even from people who don't believe Coggers was/is haunted, who told me, they heard footsteps behind them, following them, stopping when they stopped and continuing on when they did.

Stephen Sousa was with me a couple times when Coggers decided "to go off" as I call it. Once he and I were having a fire at the bottom of the hill by Wightman Street one fall night. We couldn't have been more then 12 or 13 at the time, but that night, with a fire going, we were scared. Whether it was because of our adulthood approaching or another reason, when we met and talked about it, we found that we remembered being scared for different reasons. A

As I sit and gather the cloak of my memories and draw it about me, I clearly remember the darkness of that night, all around us, the brightness of the fire, and us discussing being freaked out a bit. We both felt like we were being watched. I remember having a stick we had collected, that had a nice hook in it and telling him, "well, I got my neck stick and if anyone comes to kill us, I'm gonna swing this right at his neck!" And I swung my flaming brand through the air. Age and memory makes him claim the neck stick as his own, I know better but I will give it to him. As we talked and remembered that night, he blew my mind as he recounted his side of the story. I remember that I had been hearing noises up on the hill behind us, people walking and leaves moving. It really sounded like a person was walking around up there, being creepy, watching us, but not coming down, just lurking. This went on for an hour or so,(hence the neck stick), and as we talked about the noises we were hearing coming from the woods, my friend Eric came running down the hill screaming, trying to scare us. He succeeded. Initially, I felt relieved since I knew that what I was hearing was him, but as we talked, he told me he had seen someone else up on the hill, not moving, not saying anything to anyone. Just there.

Coggers.

Steve said, "*I was hearing noises towards Brownie Hill, the leaves rustling, the clicking, like someone pounding on a tree. But it could've been anybody, or anything. People hung out down there.*"

I agreed with him. Lord knows I hung out down there, but people didn't hang around in the dark on a fall night, watching people. I didn't remember hearing anything from the area of Brownie Hill, never mind clicking. When he said that, I thought of Katrina and I and I realized how lucky a couple of young teens were that night. We never knew what or who was watching us, up on the hill that we all heard and Eric saw. It could've been a person, could be a spirit, who knows what was around us that night.

Steve also told me he used to hear the footsteps following him, and stopping when he stopped. Like he said to me, *"usually you would freak yourself out to the point where you just booked it and ran for your life."*

Booked it. I love that phrase. In my neighborhood it meant run as fast as you could, as in, "it's my parents, book it!"

One summer night we were with a mutual friend at the party spot on Brownie Hill. Our friend and I had smoked a joint and Steve was drinking a beer. We were there, talking and laughing, when I heard a noise coming from the beach. Remember, I knew these woods like the back of my own hand. Whenever I heard anything, my mind located where it was coming from. That night, it was the beach. To me, it sounded like ten people were talking and laughing, I recognized it, thought to myself, "They are at the beach drinking" and dismissed it and went back to my conversation. All of a sudden, Steve looked at me and said, "Do you hear that?"

Steve:

"I don't remember background noise, I don't remember anything else, all of sudden it was there. I heard it, and instantly,

I thought, this ain't right, this is nothing that's supposed to be here now."

"No, you're right, it was such a freaky noise, and it didn't do it once, it didn't do it twice," I said,

"It kept doing it," Steve said.

"You were always such a tough kid. You said, come on man, let's go check it out, and I said, fuck you dude, I'm not going to find out what that thing is, and you said come on, there's two of us, and I said, listen to that thing, you think it's worried about two nineteen-year-old kids?" I reminisced.

"I'm sorry, I always wore my balls on my shoulder," Steve laughed.

What we heard that night, as we sat there, and talked and laughed was pretty scary. Like I said, to me, it started sounding like people were talking way off in the distance, and as I talked to Steve, it changed. It changed into a repetitive screaming noise, so loud and so odd sounding, that it scared the hell out of us. Steve stopped me mid conversation and said, "Dude, do you hear that?" and we listened. Whatever it was,was screaming from the trail that wrapped behind the hill. And as we all stopped and paid attention to it, our mutual friend, (that I haven't been able to locate) got all bug eyed and wanted to leave. Steve wanted to go investigate. And me, recognizing what I was feeling, (Katrina, the dog, every other time I was chased out of the woods) talked him out of it. I remember saying, "Let's get out of here."

"Why? There are two of us." He thrust his chin out

"Steve, listen to that thing, do you think it's going to be scared by the two of us?" I asked.

"Guys, let's get out of here, I don't like it." My friend Janet said.

Steve looked at me a moment longer, listening to this, "Coggers Creature," scream and then saw the logic of my advice. We hiked out, me leading the way, Steve bringing up the rear, ready to fight. Whatever it was, screamed the whole time we walked out.

That's what it was, a scream.

Andy Laderoute was one of my closest friends as a kid. He and I played together almost all the time and explored our area. We raised hell on a daily basis and had a great time doing it. Andy is a great guy, someone I will always consider a friend, but down to earth, certainly not given to flights of fancy. When I was writing this, I harassed him a few times and he basically told me, "I never had anything happen to me down there."

I assumed it was because he had a somewhat normal family, and hence wasn't sensitive to anything. But while chatting on Facebook one night, he mentioned a couple of odd things he remembered that I didn't. I immediately got together with him and he, well, he blew my mind away.

"One time we were coming from McDonald's or something and as we walked down the path we came across that big old pine tree there, it was covered with bras and panties," he remembered.

"What? I don't remember that at all." I truly didn't remember it.

"Come on man, you don't remember that? Someone must have stolen a ton of stuff from Caldor's,(a local store). We stood

there and laughed and took some down and started screwing around, putting them on and laughing," he explained.

"Not at all man, not at all." I crinkled my brow as I tried to recall, vaguely I remembered something, but no clear memory.

"That's when we heard that thing," he said.

"What thing?" All ears, I perked up.

"We were joking around and laughing and throwing bras at each other and we heard that noise," he said.

"What did it sound like?" I asked.

"Well, that's what was funny. To me it sounded like an animal growling, to you, you said it sounded different, that's what I remember about it. In fact, that's why I remember it, because we both heard something different," he told me.

"What did we do?" I asked mystified. I honestly didn't remember this.

"We looked around and couldn't see anything, and then we went back to throwing them around and laughing, joking that maybe we had offended a God of the tree or something (definitely my humor) and we heard it again."

"Are you shitting me dude?"

"No, this time it was louder and closer and we got scared and we ran."

This one story blew my mind because I didn't remember it at all, and it was also perfect, because how many times had me and others heard something and it sounded different to all of us.

"I was also creeped out by the path by Cashin Street. That's the only place that really scared me at night down Coggers. Sometimes I would hear footsteps behind mine and I would run."

Since that's where we have gotten a ton of EVP's (Electronic Voice Phenomena …more on them later), a surprise. I guess he's a lot more sensitive than I gave him credit for.

One of my friends Paula put it pretty succinctly I always felt watched when i knew no one was there. I would feel eyes on me all the time, loud bangs and foot steps. There would be nothing there to make those noises, that's a lot of the reason I would call on you to hang out or go fishing.

Lauri McTeague grew up on the street next to mine. She was a bright, pretty young woman, and someone that we all had a crush on.

It was a place not like any other in the city. I actually lived on top of a pond, Cogger's Pond to be exact. It was a pond with high banks, which made for great sledding onto the ice in the winter. It was a place surrounded by trees and trails. It was great for cut-throughs to other places. It was great in the daytime, but cutting through at nighttime would leave a chill up your spine. It could be the whistling of the trees or the eerie feeling of someone or something always behind you. No matter what it was, it definitely would put an extra hop in your step.

When my childhood friend, Norman Shaw popped up on Facebook and asked me to recall some of these childhood memories, I was at first taken aback, because I think I put those memories in a far away compartment. Then I started to actually think about my childhood and some weird things that had happened. When I was carrying age, the age when my mother would carry me up to bed, I remember looking over her shoulder and out into our backyard and seeing something. It was something that glided across the back yard, transparent and howling. I remember squeezing my mom so tight and closing my eyes all the way up the stairs. That was my first experience and not my last. As I mentioned in the beginning, I always felt something as I would cut through the yard into the trails. Something there.

The house I grew up in was built in the late 1890's, during the industrial revolution. The upper third of the street has houses of that age. My father grew up in the house and I believe his father did too.

One more strange note, is that there have been some drownings in the pond and some stories of the pond being a bottomless pit with no known depth. It was always mysterious growing up. Now, when I go home and see development around the pond, I am saddened by what once was a cool, yet eerie place, surrounded by modular homes and retirement communities.

Good stuff! These are just the few that I've been able to contact after 20 or so years of not talking. I wish I could have gotten in contact with some of the others.

Researching the land, looking and trying to figure out WHY it was haunted like it was, what made it so screwed up. I came across some interesting things, but then again, we haven't even talked about the reform school yet.

CHAPTER 5

The Middlesex County Training School was on Princeton Boulevard in Chelmsford. The main driveway ran parallel with Wightman Street, the street next to mine. The rest of the land sprawled into Coggers; it took the bulk of the lower right part of the rough triangle that was Coggers woods. Though there were a few houses that ran along Princeton Boulevard on the same side of the street as the school, behind them was the land owned by the state, Training School Property. The whole place was fenced in and that's what you noticed first as you drove or walked past. It was this fence running alongside Princeton Boulevard, and while it wasn't topped with barbed wire or anything, it gave the impression of, "stay out."The only part that was semi inviting was the main driveway since it ran smack dab into a brick building that looked like pain, it obviously didn't get many visitors. To the right of this access and behind the fence was a huge area of rushes and grass, with two small ponds dropped in for good measure. I remember fishing in there a few times as a kid, but I don't think I ever caught anything, except bad feelings. This marshy looking wetland was teeming with life in the

Springand Summer as brown heads burst forth from the green shoots that then turned a diffuse golden color in the Fall and Winter. It was a couple of hundred yards wide and maybe a half-mile long. It tapered to a point and ended and turned into hillside. This hill was shaped like a "J" and ran behind the rushes and was covered with oaks and maples. For half the year, the training school's imposing buildings were hidden from view by them, and in the winter you could glimpse them standing like sentinels. It was a huge facility of red brick buildings topped with slate shingled roofs and spread along the hilltop that gently rose a quarter of a mile in. Everything about it said, "Institution", and "bad days."

    Meandering in and among the buildings were roads and parking lots, and while walking along them, you wonder what the hell were they thinking of when they paved them. At the very tippity top of the hill was a great white gazebo standing alone in a parking lot. It was here that Eric Costa and I were caught by security when I was about 12 and I was called, "a young adult," when he referred to me in his walkie-talkie. Behind the gazebo and buildings, the hill dropped steeply off to its endless fields that touched into Coggers. Down there was a baseball diamond with rusty chain link backstops and a football field where historic games took place on windy fall afternoons. We seldom went down into those fields, unless it was with a purpose such as to play football or continue exploring along the Route 4 part of Coggers. Since they were so steep, those hills were great sledding as a kid when we felt motivated enough to hike back there.

    The Training School was built in 1894 from land purchases by Percy Parker and Henry Ferrin by the state. That original institution was considered a success and more land was purchased in the 1890's, 1900's and in the 1930's. Eventually it would comprise 42 acres and eight large buildings and assorted outbuildings. It was officially known as the Middlesex County Truancy School. From the late 1890's to the early 1970's, if you were a kid ages 7 to 16 who got into trouble, or one who skipped school and got caught a lot, you had a one in three chance of ending up here.

I think of that now, seven. Let's put an exclamation point after that seven! Hell, let's put a bunch of them…7!!!!!!! A seven year old kid, taken from home, sent to live with a bunch of other strangers in some giant buildings where the only people who took care of you were people who couldn't even spell the words, "childhood development". SEVEN !!!!!!!!!!!!!!!!

Its population ran anywhere from 60 to 150 kids at any one time. In the beginning, it was praised as an institution where troubled youths learned to behave, while being taught school and responsibilities. They grew vegetables, had a band and marched in the annual Chelmsford Fourth of July parade every year until its closing. Near the end, it was a place of employment for the cronies of the political hacks of the era, and if stories are to be believed, the employees would get drunk across the street at the local watering hole and go back and beat on the kids. While researching it, I came across numerous praises for it in the local paper, all in the 1930's and 1950's. Then the tale starts to get a bit darker.

For me, my earliest memory was being sent there to learn how to swim in a summer camp. I don't recall how young I was, all I knew was that I didn't want to be there and I cried a lot. My memory flash of me crying, waiting to go swimming, wearing one of those stupid looking foam balls strapped to my back, (to save me from drowning I guess,) sums up the whole place to me. I also see images of me fishing with other kids as a child. I think my parents sent me to a day camp one year, (maybe they were mad at me). I also remember going to a 4-H fair held there with my sisters. The excitement of the word, "fair," had brought delightful images of Ferris wheels and big soft cotton candy balls to waste my teeth away on. Walking home with two stupid plants in my hands and a confused look on my face, reminds me to never go to a 4-H fair as long as I live again.

    No matter who you are, how old you are or what your belief systems are, if you stood on Princeton Boulevard and looked at that place, you would say, "it's creepy," or "I don't like the look of it," because it is creepy. It gives off a horrible vibe that makes you think of skinned knees and broken bottles. I know now that places can retain the emotions of what's happened there, especially if they are strong. Well, the Training School was that place. Here are some examples of strong emotion. In 1957, a brave ex-Marine quit his job there as a cottage supervisor. His name was Hugh C. Duffy. He made a report to the district attorney's office that the supervisors there were beating the kids. Using three foot broom handles, he asserted they used arrogance and violence to keep the kids in line.

There were a few other articles about Hugh Duffy, ultimately, very little came of his allegations.

In 1965, Carl Earle died on Princeton Boulevard, in front of the Middlesex Training School when his scooter crashed and he was thrown. In 1972, the Lowell Sun did a three day back page expose on the school. This is where we get the best information of what it was like to live there.

Sad to say I was happy when I came across this article in the paper, it was shortly afterwards that it was ordered closed.

"I saw a kid named Larry (not his real name) get handcuffed by his hands behind his back by Mr. B. Then Mr. B brought Larry into a closet, shut the door, and beat Larry over the head with a broom, punched and kicked him in the face. When Larry came out of the closet, he was dragged out by his hair. He had blood all over his face and he was crying.

"I got beat up a lot of times while I was at Middlesex for smoking cigarettes, swearing and running away."

"The kids are not allowed to smoke cigarettes. One day I was down in the locker room smoking one and this guy, Mr. X, came down and busted me. He put the cigarette out and started slapping me across the face with his hands. Then he put me on line to write," I will not smoke as long as I am at the Middlesex County Training School." "I had to do this for 15 days. I had to stand up writing from about 8:00 a.m. till 9:00 p.m. for the whole 15 days. The only time I got to sit down was during lunch time. I had to wear this long nightshirt during the whole 15 days. Then about four days after I was off line I got busted with matches. You're not allowed to have matches there either. Mr. W. busted me that time and I had to do another 15 days on the line, this time writing, "I will not carry matches while at the Middlesex County Training School."

"I ran away while on line because I couldn't take standing there and writing there anymore. So this one day I just jumped out the window. About a month later the police picked me up. They took me back to Middlesex. The first thing that happened when I got back was I got a haircut, a whiffle, that's a baldie. They're not supposed to give haircuts there."

"Then Mr. W. took me into the locker room downstairs and beat me up. He punched me in the face, slapped me and swore at me for 15 minutes. Then he brought me upstairs and I was on the line again, this time for 30 days this time writing ,"I will not run away from the Middlesex County Training School" for 30 days, once again standing in the same nightshirt. You can't talk to anybody and nobody can talk to you when you're on line. I had to write at least 2,000 lines each day."

"I couldn't take standing on line again for another 30 days, so I ran again. A month later, I got picked up by the police and returned to Middlesex. This time the first thing that happened was Mr. A and Mr. B beat me up, punching, slapping and kicking me for about a half hour."

Imagine standing all day, in a nightshirt, writing the same sentences over and over again. Yes, some of us had to do that in school. Now imagine doing it from breakfast to bedtime, for five days. Try to do it for one day, I dare you, and see how you feel. Try doing it for a week and you would be half insane.

One boy reported that the classroom work was too difficult for him. Because he couldn't do any of the work, he was put on line frequently. He requested a transfer to another group. When that was refused he threatened to run away. In response, "Mr Z. told one of the masters to bring me over to Richardson Cottage and handcuff me to a door, standing up. I was handcuffed to the horizontal pole you push the door open with. I was handcuffed about 3:00 in the afternoon, standing up, and had to stay there until bedtime. I wasn't allowed to eat dinner or anything. At bedtime, I was removed from the door, taken to my locker to change into my nightshirt. Then I was brought over to my bed and handcuffed by one hand to the bedpost. The next day I was handcuffed to the same door again, standing up. That night I was once again handcuffed to the bed. The following day they removed the handcuffs and I ran."

Can you blame him? Can anyone?

"When you run a lot, the staff makes you put on a nightie with nothing on underneath and stand outside in the playground writing on some paper supported by a board, writing," I will not run away from the Middlesex County Training School anymore because I like it here." "Nobody ever talks to you, just about, and *you can't ever talk to anybody. They have no counselors, no social workers, no one to talk to when something's on your mind, when something's bothering you. In a way it makes you think about wanting to kill them when you get out. You start getting awfully lonely. It really makes you want to run and that's why I did it. It drives you crazy up there."*

    May God help heal their souls. This institution, built in the 1890's, was supposed to take troubled youths and help make them men. Well, personally from what I've seen, it did make them men, screwed up men who graduated and went on to commit more crimes. And while that is a broad assertion, it's one that has basis in fact. When searching on Google, I came across tons of court transcripts where the defendants in cases had spent time there. Is this surprising? Not to me. Even if we take Mr. Hugh Duffy's report as an isolated incident, you still have years and years of physical and mental abuse. Given the ages, it is surprising that with hundreds if not thousands of kids suffering abuse, people who see the place think it's creepy. Out of everyone I've talked to as an adult who grew up in my neighborhood, no one liked the place. More surprisingly given the amount of woods, not one of us, NOT ONE, can ever remember seeing an animal there, or even a bird. It is a creepy, horrible place. It just looks and feels like pain in the shape of red brick buildings. As a kid, I was totally oblivious to it, and it served its purpose of being an area for my friends and I to explore. Though none of us liked it, we would often be found scouring the outbuildings for things to break or play with, (most likely break). Never alone though. I don't ever remember going there alone unless it was a quick ride through on my bike. When I was about 10, one of the group discovered something extremely interesting to us.Since the Training School was surrounded by fence on three sides, (front and sides) and it was bordered by Cogger's, one of the more enterprising of us had found an opening in the fence near Brownie Hill. We could walk down into Coggers and cross into the Training School there and come up behind it. That was the path of least resistance since sometimes walking up the road in our searches for things to break, we would be told kindly to, "get the hell out of here," by gruff looking security guards,.

Someone, to this day I don't know who,(nor do I believe the many claims I've heard over the years), discovered a wooden slat crate. You know the kind, thin strips of wood about six inches wide, held together with wire. Since this was a sizable object, it was roughly hauled into Coggers before being opened. Inside were four ammunition cases. Each was labeled, "Property of US Government 7.62mm rounds." Opening these with dreams of belts of machine gun ammo, we found two shoulder strap Army green pouches. It was the perfect kind of thing for carrying loose rounds in. A riddle inside a riddle. At the time, we didn't stop and think or wonder, we just made daily forays to the Training School to get more cases. Every day we went down and brought another friend to show them what we had found, and everyday another crate of these cases went over the fence. We quickly depleted the supply of 30 or so cases stacked behind the outbuilding we were raiding.

I remember one particularly hot summer day when my friend Terry, (brother of the three foot long snot kid,) found a round in one. It was brand new and it gleamed in the mid day sun. I was all for building a fire and throwing it in (I told you I was stupid then,), but my friend's wiser head prevailed and he gave it to Mr. Thomas, the Local cop who lived on our street. Mr. Thomas asked where we had found it, and either he was a bad cop, (very doubtful), or our reply of,"on the street," convinced him. Personally, I think he was ready to let the matter close since the bullet looked like it had just come from the production line and not the ground.

After using up all of the cases, we started exploring the other out buildings. We came across sheds where they stored the rock salt used in the winter. Since it was built into a hillside, we took great delight in ripping off shingles and breaking them up into smaller pieces and spinning them off. Because of their flatness, they would often break at extreme angles and we all howled with laughter when we started throwing them at each other. You remember the old reel to reel computers? I don't remember how or why or when, but we once got into a building in the back and took great delight in throwing reels of old computer tape down the hillside. These things were huge, at least a foot across and the tape was thick. At the time, we didn't question why they would have these things, like all kids, we merely reacted. This sudden plunder was quickly forgotten once it was broken. Sometimes we would break into the big buildings, since at that time, many of them were abandoned. Ten fingers were usually required to give the boost to the second floor window. Always white halls, always in decay and always creepy. Sometimes a desk might sit by itself in the middle of a room, most often it was empty, but I think even as kids, we were freaked out by the place.

Whether we picked up on the vibe there or not, there wasn't a lot of exploring. When I was about 13, my good friend Steve Sousa climbed into the second floor and as he leaned over to help me up, he jabbed a great big shard of glass in his leg. Straight in it went and straight down Steve came. After pulling it out like Arthur and sword, blood started gushing. Personally, I thought that was pretty cool, as any wound deep enough to bleed hard was sure to leave a scar. I remember him leaning on me as I helped him limp to his grandmother's house, hoping none of our friends' parents saw us. My cries of, "put salt on it, put salt on it," were quickly hushed there, and I was sent home while Steve went to the hospital.

During my late teens as I bumped into my old friends less and less frequently, when we did, we would often talk of the ammo cases and computer reels and wonder what they were doing there. It led to some great speculation, especially with the hauntings and other stuff we found. It was only recently that I found they were teaching the kids how to be soldiers in the 1960's. As most of you know, during the 60's if you got caught doing a crime, you were given a choice. Doing time here or doing time in Vietnam as a soldier. I am sure the logic was they thought that most of the kids would return to criminal life and it only made sense to get a head start and train them to be soldiers.

When I was about 24, I ran into a neighborhood acquaintance, Dickie Hows. I say acquaintance because at some point Dickie or "Peekie"as we called him, (I have no idea how he got the name, but we can guess), was charged with assaulting a minor and is currently listed as sexual offender in Lowell. I wouldn't call him a friend, as he was older then us by about five or so years, but I was glad to see him when I was younger since he was from the neighborhood, (and hadn't committed his crime yet). One Saturday when I was at his house we started talking about Cogs and he told me what he knew about the Training School. According to him, there were a lot of people killed out there. They would be beaten, listed as runaway, then buried on site. Now how much of this is part lore and legend and grains of truth, we will never know, since all the records are kept by the state and they are sealed. I do know a childhood friend of mine, who is not into the supernatural, telling me he felt sure someone was buried there. "I was walking my dog and he was running in the meadow when all of a sudden I felt like someone was buried there," he said.

"What do you mean buried there? Like someone was murdered?"

"Yes, it was so strong. I wanted to go home and get a shovel. I had to stop myself and wonder what I was doing. That's what I remember about the training school."

In my research, I came across many accounts of investigations that were called for and done by the state. Of course, there is no mention of what they found. It was during 1973 that State Representative Paul Tsongas called for a closing of the facility, and by 1974 it was done. Afterwards, it became a rehabilitation center for the remnants of the flower children era, (imagine the spirits feeding off of that crap), and then a girls' reform school, (how we used to walk along the fence and look with longing at the buildings and dream). Then it was abandoned for a few years and the ideas flowed fast and furious what to do with it. Major corporations bid on it, submitted ideas to the town and then walked away. Then the University of Lowell bought it in the mid 1980's and it had a sign out front, "ULOWELL EAST CAMPUS." Somehow, this plan of turning it into a college campus never got off the ground, so it sat there, gently rotting away with the school using some of the buildings. In the mid1990's, a developer bought some of the land and built retirement homes. If you were over 55 you could retire to the lovely haunted Training School grounds. Part of this deal was that a large chunk of Coggers next to it was also sold, and he lopped off the top of Brownie hill and built houses there.

I worked with my step-dad pouring the concrete floors for those houses. Each day we would show up to the job and say, "it's a fucking shame," and go and pour concrete. Every time we showed up, another chunk of Coggers would be gone, or more cleared out. Each time we would shake our heads, and go to work. Hey, I needed money. Every year after, another piece of the Training School would be gone, or another piece of Coggers, as more and more land was developed. Until all that remained was the pond and some of the woods close to Drum Hill Road and the Original Training School buildings and its environs. Lately, the idea is to turn the Training School into low cost housing, which would be a damn shame in so many different ways.

CHAPTER 6

The land that came to be known as Coggers was originally owned by Jerathmell Bowers, who could probably trace his family back to the Mayflower. Originally, the city of Lowell was a part of Chelmsford. It was only a land grant in 1826 that Lowell was incorporated first as a town, then in 1836 as a city. The earliest reference to good ole Jerathmell (what a great 1700 name, Jerathmell, if I ever have another son, I will name him that) is in 1702.

"Monday Oct 26th 1702. Went to Chelmsford, by that time got there 'twas almost dark, saw Captain Bowers and his company; gave a volley and huzza'ssup'd at Mr. Clark's and Colonel Pierce in his study."

Samual Sewall VOL II p.67

Ha-ha, what great writing of those times. Sup'd, huzzahs and volleys, good stuff. Please bear with me as I try and trace this land to the modern day and whilst doing so, entertain you, so please don't you throw this down out of sheer boredom, or fall asleep while reading it. When researching this, I found that looking for land records and deeds was much like sticking pins through your fingers, possible, but not fun. This was so painful, so disheartening, that sometimes I thought about just writing this section as, "the land was there since I can remember."

Jerathmell was granted a license for making, "strong waters," as long as he didn't sell them to the Indians (yes I said Indians, and not more PC Native Americans). When he died a couple years later his sons "Jerathmell and John Fisk "were also granted license to do so. We find the land being handed down to family over and over again as the years pass. We see the original homestead of hundreds, if not thousands of acres being sold, bit by bit, as the city develops and spreads. We don't find many references to Coggers except as, "swamp." The first real hit I came across, (and I didn't, a lovely woman friend of mine did), was a map from the 1800's showing Coggers roughly where it was when I was a kid. It was surrounded by roads in roughly the same position, and there were these cool little lines with plants and icons that denote swampland there. I looked at it and said, "Holy shit, it was swampy even then, "and as I checked out the map some more, I realized it's always been in that triangle. That the roads that I knew and know, had been there roughly there for hundreds of years. That kind of set me back. Instinctively I thought to myself, "this area has been forbidden for a long time, "and it reinforced what I thought. Also, it could have just been they didn't really like to build roads through a swamp or even close to it, but I like the eerie scary version better.

And there I sat for many many months. I couldn't find anything about the land, despite what you hear to the contrary and the Chelmsford Historical Society isn't really any help at all. So I stood at an impasse for a long time. I knew the original house that owned most of Lowell, The Bowers place. I knew where it was and what it looked like, I had banged on the door a few times, (no answer), but digging through handwritten records from the 1700's was impossible. Seriously, "Yeoman Smith, bought a parcel of land 200 rods north of the old pine tree to the stone bound near the brook that stopped existing 100 years ago," kind of thing. I did this for a couple of days and started doubting my own sanity. I contemplated giving up, but then one night, as I sat at the Lowell Library perusing microfilm of old newspapers, looking for parts to this book ,(after two hours of that, you're dizzy and numb to the point of stupidity), I took another look at the City Atlas of Lowell that laid on top of the microfilm racks. And with that flash of understanding that sometimes strikes, I realized there were four different atlases there. Starting in the 1870's and ending in 1936. It was there that I was able to see the owners of Coggers through a span of years. As I read the 1936 edition, I saw, "P Coggers," delineated at the end of Wightman Street. I did a backflip, calmed the library staff down when they picked me up off of the floor and went back to looking. So, Coggers was named after Coggers, but how did he go from owning a little slice between the Training School and Corey Street? It was obvious that the land he owned was small, while the rest was still listed as Bowers. But as I stood there, flipping and examining the atlases and reading the names, they reached through history to me saying, "It's about time you moron!" And with this info, I was able to go to the Registry of Deeds in Lowell and hit pay dirt.

After harassing one of the civil servants who work there, for the 200th time, I actually found something to chew on. It was sad in a way, because what I originally found was Jesse Bowers, (the owner of the land in the 1940's), having land taken by the city of Lowell for non-payment of taxes. When I saw this, I thought, "Holy crap, he must have owed some serious coin for them to take land."No, the city took 44 dollars worth of land from him. Ha-ha, 44 dollars worth of land would amount to a six inchdiameter area now. Even in the 1940's it wasn't much, but still, it served to show me the straits this man and his wife were in. But I get off track. The land went from Jerathmell Bowers, the original owner to his son Jerathmell, and then from Jerathmell to HIS son Jonathan and Jonathan died in 1756.

Yes 1756, this isn't Europe. When I read that I said, "Holy shit, 1756." And he left massive amounts of land to his son, Francis Bowers, who deeded the Coggers portion to his brother William in 1795. When William made his will and testament, he reserved a life estate for his wife Hannah and himself, and in turn granted the land to his son Joseph in 1809. They both died in 1815 and Joseph owned the land for the next 50 years. I was going to skip over this, but when I pointed out that I thought "reserved a life estate for himself,"was strange to a friend, she said, "I would think a lot of people do that."

"What? I don't think so, this was the old days."I replied being somewhat angry that she was 86'ing my theory that I was going to put in the book.

"Especially in the old days, you would gift your land away, but didn't want your evil kids booting you off when they sold it down the road."She smugly stated back.

I was irritated,"Watch where you're driving."

"You don't think it's odd, when a few generations do it?"I was grumpy.

"No," she didn't

Dammit, here I was thinking that in the old days something happened on the land and old man Francis said to his brother, "now there Joe, cause all those people died, and because of all the witchcraft our family practiced here on this land, you gotta keep it in the Bowers clan, lest any evil be unleashed on mankind or on little kids that want to play in the woods roun' here."And Joe, being a good man, replied, "Yes, I agree Francis, how long do you think it will be till the land will forget the deeds you folks have done?" No such luck, but we do find a few generations of Bowers making it clear, "I'm staying here till I'm good and dead."Francis held the land for a long time till he in turn, granted it to his brother Joseph.

Joseph deeded the land to his son Sewall, in 1854, and of course he and his wife had, "life estates there." If you Google, "Sewall Bowers," you will come up with all sorts of hits and info. Most of it is useless, especially if you're trying to write a book about the haunted woods that exists on land he used to own. Anyway, Sewall and his wife Sylvia lived there a long time and deeded the land to their son Joseph, (creative names obviously didn't run in the family), in the 1880's. When he died in 1893, his wife must have been pretty happy, because instead of following him like most wives do, she outlived him and lived on the property till 1902. That's when Joseph Bowers got it and in turn granted it to his son Jesse in 1926, and that was the name that I found in the 1936 city atlas of Lowell. I can't express how happy I was to see the property on a map, with a name attached, and feel like I was getting somewhere, (it was at this point I realized how lame my life was becoming). I felt like tap dancing when I found him in the Registry of Deeds a few days later. As I said before, the first item I discovered was the city taking some of the land away, and as I read that, even as broke as I am, I wished I could have given them the 44 dollars. So here we have this old family, who at one point, owned most of Lowell. Slowly and slowly the family fortunes turn, they become less and less wealthy, and less and less able to pay for everything they own.

As I dug in the records even more, I found Joseph mortgaging land to Patrick Cogger.

Ah hah, and in December of 1944, we see Jesse and his wife Amy, signing the land over to William P Coggers. Perusing around, I had found Jesse mortgaging the land in the 1930's to Coggers. Eventually, they couldn't keep up with it, and signed it over. What a nice Christmas present for them! Reading it, I could feel the heaviness of it. I could feel the frustration and to be honest, I felt a little sad for the family. After that, I found Coggers mortgaging it, along with other properties in 1952, to the tune of $32,000 dollars, a hefty chunk back then. It was this that led me to think, "ok, so he gets the land, mortgages it, and then opens the gravel pit",(I won't tell you the number of times I had come across Ads for 'P.Coggers Sand and Gravel' in the back of microfilmed newspaper and went cuckoo trying to find something out, all to no avail.). So, there I stood, at a place where I had finally found out the reason for the damn name, but not the how. Being thickheaded and obnoxious, I kept digging. The same day I found out about the title and land transfers, I went to the library, and as I stood at the microfilm racks I thought to myself, "ok, so Coggers gets the land and mortgages it, and opens the gravel pit in 1952, by 1957-58 he had to have hit water." So I took out the months for 1958 and at the end of a long session where I was falling asleep and wanting to burn the microfilm stacks to the ground, I found it. I found a report in the Lowell Sun showing that the city council was concerned with how steep the hillsides were, and they were talking about fencing it off, to keep people from falling in and drowning. Then a few days later in the newspaper, I found a picture of it taken in 1958 and it showed how it looked back then. I could clearly see my old neighbor's house; clearly see everything the way it used to be. It was the brass ring I had spent months searching for. I seriously doubt anyone at the library had ever seen a patron so excited over the Lowell Sun 1950's years.

There my research stands. I couldn't find out any other things that happened to the land. All the trails died with Coggers in the 1950's. I had found lots of references to it in the Lowell Sun, but no more deeds. That night, as I added my latest acquisitions to the pile of microfilm prints I had from the newspaper, I realized I had dug up quite a lot of information from there. Some of it was what I considered, "gems," while others was me printing stuff off out of sheer desperation of trying to feel like I accomplished something. I had spent many hours at the library drifting through the newspapers, looking for info. If I could have found one headline, "killer Coggers takes lives again," I would still be there looking now, since that is ideal for this. But reality was far different. It really was a needle in a haystack thing. I knew. I KNEW there had to be some references to it. Hell, I knew as a 12 year old, that someone drowned in the pond so I should be able to find that! I knew the Training School was opened in the late 1800's, so there are constant references to it throughout the years in the Lowell Sun. But that was illusion, I knew I wasn't going to find "15 kids beat to death at Middlesex Country Reform School" even if it was true. I knew I had to find some meat and potatoes; some deaths listed in the paper, some horrible things to happen, to tie what I knew and felt in Coggers, to the real world. My friend's mom told him she remembered someone drowning there in the 1940's, so I spent hours and hours going through the 1940's. First the summer months, then the winter months, (hey people drown in winter too, thin ice). My lack of success led me to despair and scary feelings. Sometimes as I scanned through I began to get hopeful when I saw, "heat wave," or smile when I saw, "local boy drowns." Because I knew, if there was a heat wave in the spring, chances are, someone would drown, and it might be my nugget. How sad is that? I actually found myself wondering if I was going crazy reading microfilm. So from there I bounced to the1980's, looking for Larry Cox, a teen who I personally knew, and one who drowned in Coggers.

After 3 weeks of staring at microfilm, I came across this, it brought me a lot of happiness

As I thought of Larry, I remember fishing without any luck, soon afterwards and thinking with a 12 year olds innocence, "are they full from chomping on him?"Unfortunately, I didn't remember the exact year he died and I started searching in the early 80's. After days of mind numbing searching and no luck, I was excited to come across references to the Training School, to Coggers. The developers argued with each other and the towns tried to come up with ideas on how to use these great old buildings. I was so happy to at least find something in a newspaper related to the woods that I eagerly printed these off. I would look at them, and say, "Cool, I found something." The articles sat in a pile."Training School to be surveyed," or, "No plans yet for training school property." There they still sit, useless, a reminder of the effort this took. Then one day I found it. June 8, 1985, "Lowell Man Drowns in Pond." I was so excited I yelled, "Yeah," and raised my fist in victory, only to be hushed by the librarian. My victory was complete when I read in the article, "when police asked, they were told the name of the pond was Coggers." Then I asked, "Nice, now we know there is a reason for it to be called Coggers, but why?" That, "why," led me to the search for "William P Coggers."

But here at least, was a means for one spirit to be there. I know and knew there was more than one down there. Hell, from what I felt, there were hundreds of spirits there, but here was a valid reason for the masses, (**YOU**), to accept. I know spirits are everywhere, unfortunately for my book sales, others don't. So I dug for proof. I tried everything I could. There are programs to search newspaper archives, (bad at best), and they led me to articles of, "Training School Band plays in local parade," and other useless things to me. Until one day I was perusing the papers in the 1973, I came across an article talking about how the Ex Headmaster of the Training School was still living there, and had been asked to leave. AHAH! So digging in 1972, I finally chanced upon the Lowell Sun's expose on the Training School, and other bits relating to how horrible it really was. Flashing through hundreds of pages of newspapers and stopping on an article relating to Coggers or the Training School, you can say, "Chance," to me, but there is no chance.

      So that's what I've dug up. I would love to be able to type this and say, "Yeah man, I found hundreds of deaths and reports of witchcraft and horror, maybe some good ole Indian slaughter thrown in for good measure." No, that isn't reality as much as I might want it to be. I am thankful for what I have found because all in all, it is important, and I was lucky to find out the Training School was the hellhole I imagined it being. It was rewarding to find out that someone did drown in the pond and there are reasons for the spirits to be there, and most of all, to find out why it was called Coggers.

      To me, it was from the 1950's on that it was relevant. That's when the pond was created and people had a chance of drowning.

Top Photo is of one of the Bowers Grave
Below is from the 1930s of the Original House

Top Photo is the view from the top of the hill as it is today
Below is a photo of the Training School

Top Photo is from the top of the hill in the Spring of 1994
Below is looking straight ahead from the top of the hill 1994

Top Photo is looking towards the party spot in Autumn of 1992
Below is at water edge from the same time period

Top Photo Hugh Duffy holds the broomstick used to beat children
Below Gentle criticism indeed

Top Photo is from the 1950s right after they hit water
Below thrown from a scooter, he died in front
of the Training School

The End was drawing near when the Sun ran this expose

The state agreed shortly thereafter

BOOK 2

CHAPTER 7

So I lived my life. I grew up, graduated and started working full time. As I got older and older, I stopped going to Coggers, all the time. Time passed as it does and my friends got apartments. The old, "what should we do?" was replaced with, "let's go to your house." The spirit world never left me alone though. Every place I lived in was haunted, nothing like Coggers, not that intense. No, these were hauntings that seemed to follow me around, and if it didn't follow me around, well I had a unique talent for picking places to live in. As a young 20-something, I began to notice a presence of something that hung around me. It was that disquieting feeling of not being alone, of being watched all the time, something intangible yet noticeable. Lying in bed at night, sometimes I would feel my blankets move, or something sit down next to me, and I would roll over and try to ignore it. Other times, I would lay there listening to tapping from inside a one board thick wall, level with me as I lay in bed and have to tell myself, "well, it hasn't killed me yet; I guess I won't die tonight," to help me fall asleep. While my life moved on and I grew into adulthood, the spirit world never left me alone.

Eventually, I too grew up and got married and had children. The house my wife and I had was extremely haunted,(yay surprise!),and while I didn't go down to Coggers very often, my brother and I talked about it and I would always give it the hairy eyeball when I visited mom and dad's.

I would say all in all, I lived a haunted life.

Like all of us, God always kept his eye on me and didn't let me forget that he had plans that didn't take my feelings into consideration. Since I had missed, or ignored his signs up until this point, he came in like a whirlwind and changed my life for the better. Though it was very hard to see at the time, going through it, hindsight lends perspective.

I started my own business and ended up going bankrupt.

Once bankrupt, my wife divorced me.

Once divorced, I was raising my kids alone, working at a job I didn't like.

Once I was a parent, I met someone and got engaged and she got pregnant as well.

We ended up splitting up and now I had someone else who I disappointed.

So here I was, 33 years old, paying child support to someone whom I thought I was going to marry, but didn't. I was also taking care of two kids and working a job that stressed me out all day long. Everything I had tried had either failed through my own mistakes or just turned to shit somehow. I cannot describe the level of failure I felt at that time. I was so disgusted with myself and my life. Every hope of mine, wasted. The only thing I seemed good at, was whining about my bad luck and getting women to jump into bed with me. But at that point, I honestly felt, why bother with women? I will just screw it up and hurt them, and who the hell would want to be with a guy who is divorced and has three kids?

To give a good example of how low I felt, I remember once I was with the kids at the Laundromat, and there was this pretty lady sitting there. I couldn't help myself, I mean, this woman was beautiful and it was one of those "you have to tell her how pretty she is, or you're a moron" So I walked up and told her "you are one of the most beautiful women I have ever seen," and she smiled at me, and said "you should see me with my makeup on!" I mean come on, what an intro for the next "I would love to, when are you free?"

But instead I sighed and thought to myself, "I'm a divorced dad with three kids who isn't going to own a home for the next 20 years, why would anyone want to see me?" I actually thought that and I just sighed, slumped my shoulders, turned and walked away. Her laughter followed me into my truck. Imagine how she felt, some guy walks up, compliments her, and then given an opening, sighs and walks away.

At work my friends and co-workers started calling me bad luck and would joke how the crows seemed to follow me from jobsite to jobsite. The constant litany of complaining about my bad luck had begun to wear on them. Even my boss, who was making a million a year in sales from my division, was tired of me being negative. I cannot express to you how stressed out and frustrated I was, how disappointed with myself and my life. I mean my job was horrible, the attitudes, the stress of, "you can't screw this up or your ass will be fired!" the frustration I was feeling there daily was killing me. People that I knew started getting sick of my "woe is me" attitude. I would show up to job sites and just whine about life, about the job, about my lower back. Who wants to hear that? Who likes a chronic complainer? No one, especially in concrete and that's what I was.

Every single person that I knew, knew all my drama, all the sad things in my life and everything that had happened to me in the last few years. I complained to anyone who would listen, and even complained to those who wouldn't. Then when that got tiring, I complained about complaining. People would start walking away as I talked, in fact, now, I would have walked away from myself too. I was so good at playing the victim and feeding of off people's sympathy. Since all I did was focus on the negative, well, let me tell you, if there was a potential for something bad happening, it happened when I was around. My friends knew enough to keep me away during critical moments. My negativity was starting to attract bad luck to me. I've always believed in God, I always had a great faith. Ever since I was a little kid with my, "now I lay me down to sleep" prayers, (which got weird as I hit my teens and I finally learned the Lord's prayer), I've always prayed and while not a devout person of any particular faith, I've tried to do the right thing. Well, now my prayers started taking on a desperate whiny tone. "Please help me." My list of petitions to God got longer and longer till I swear my prayers would take 20 minutes. I think even God was getting sick of my whiny prayers, cause more and more things, little mundane irritating things started happening. Trust me, if something could go wrong, it did, and the spirit world? Hell, they were dancing on my head every night. I would lie in bed and hear a tap on each wall of my bedroom in the space of one second with the last coming right over my head and think, "oh crap, not tonight," or feel someone staring at me. It was simple really, more and more fear and more and more fearful things happening.

How I loved playing the victim and how I loved sympathy from people. Who doesn't want a sympathetic ear to say,"you poor thing, you deserve so much better?" after you vented frustration for 10 minutes uninterruptedly? We all do, hell even Gandhi probably did. Well, I had taken the victim to an art-form. I remember laying in bed one night praying, speaking from the heart and saying "I know I am meant to do more then pour concrete pool decks Lord, please help me."

God did.

How many crazy stories do we all have about the smallest things making the greatest of impacts on our lives? Those things are, to me, the hand of God in our lives. It's not the pillar of fire to lead the way. It's the little bird that flies by that makes you smile, or the time when I was so frustrated I said to myself, "that's it, I give up!" and then a truck with the company name "SHAW" pulls up next to me on the highway, that's God taking a moment and touching.

One night, after my usual begging, whiny prayers, I had a dream I won the lottery. Naturally I started playing the lottery every day. A few nights later, I dreamt the numbers, and man, how I raced to the store to play the lottery! I still play them, though I know the meaning of those numbers now. I actually started believing I would win the lottery. There were some days when I checked my tickets that I couldn't believe that I didn't. It was like I knew something good was coming for me, I knew it and kept checking every day. I was still complaining, but I was focusing on good for a change. I KNEW something was going to happen, I KNEW I was going to win the lottery, I didn't doubt it for a second; it was just a matter of time.

God had heard my prayers.

On a perfectly normal sunny August day, with a zero percent chance of rain, I was helping a crew pour a large stamped concrete pool deck. After we laid the concrete, I had to leave for a short time to another project, which I had managed to turn into a nightmare. Upon returning a sudden storm blew up, and it rained all over what we had just done. I distinctly remember my friend telling me, "it's your fault, and you brought it with you! You're bad luck!" My witty reply of, "fahck you," did nothing to change his mind since he sincerely thought I had brought the rain with me. Since the concrete was fairly hardened at that point, there was a chance that it might not have been damaged by this freak rainstorm; I really wasn't worried about it.

After this glorious day ended, I went to a side job I was doing and as I went to cut the concrete, I found my saw didn't work. I mean this freaking thing had just worked earlier in the morning. I started swearing and then stopped and I actually thought"maybe they are right, maybe I am bad luck."

"NO, NO WAY - THIS THING WORKS!"And after calming down I saw the cord wasn't completely plugged in, but the saw probably would've worked for anyone else.

See what I mean when I say I was jaded?

Anyway, since the work we had finished was an imprinted concrete job, it was covered with a water repellant powder. We didn't find out until the next day, after we cut and pressure washed it, that it had suffered a little damage from the rain. Being the head of the division, they sent me over to talk to the homeowner, see what the deck looked like and to take pictures.

I met our customer Tom Petrillo in his backyard. From the get go, let me say, I liked him. He was a good man with an innocent boyish face and infectious laughter. About 5'5" with glasses and dark hair, he looked like he could play an extra in, "Goodfellas," or some kid from the Bronx in "Saving Private Ryan." As we walked around and looked at not only the rain-damaged surface, but also the crappy job the guys had done cutting and power washing it, we both agreed that my company had a problem in his backyard. I complimented him on his property (always a safe bet with an angry customer) and admired the landscaping. My simple question of, "how much land do youown, "is what brings me here today. He told me that in his backyard was, "Turtle Mound," a famous Native American site that was well documented and researched. He offered to get hundreds of pages of documents he had relating to it. Jokingly I said, "I am surprised you don't have Native American Indian faces stamped into your concrete, your house must be really haunted."That right there, made him stop and listen to me, you know, really listen. He looked at me and said that it was, and that he was really into spirituality. That was the first time I had really heard and understood that word, someone who was into spirits. He took me into his house and showed me around. I got to look at his library of ghost books and check out his collection of crystals. As we walked, we chatted and he told me how he used to be a medium. In those 10 minutes, we spoke about the spirit world, Bigfoot, everything under the sun, in short, we became fast instant friends. I was caught up in the moment, here was someone who was like me, and I could talk about anything with him. I never told my co-workers my ghost stories. Come on, they're concrete workers, half of them would've made fun of me or thought I was nuts. Well, finally, here was someone who I could tell, and not only that, he wanted to hear them, indeed, he was fascinated by them. When I said, "Dude, I think there's something that's been following me around my whole life," he didn't shake his head and walk away, he looked at me, took me seriously and agreed. I had never encountered that level of acceptance in another person, and I liked it.

  I had already met his wife from when we poured the job, but we met again and we sat there and talked about something other than his crappy looking pool deck. Seriously, it was bad and I didn't want to talk about that again. I told him a few of my stories from Coggers and my life. Right away he threw it right out there, "we should start a group to investigate haunted houses."After some hemming and hawing, eventually we agreed to form our own group to investigate haunted houses, becoming rich and famous doing so. He was to be the sensitive one, and me, the scientific one. For all my fear about ghost, I was fascinated with them. I really enjoyed the good feeling that comes with connecting with someone for the first time, it had been so long.

  One of things that I found charming about Tom was that he was high energy. Everything he did was always at 1,000 miles an hour. Think about it for a moment, he just met me and already he wanted to start a group together, that was Tom.There was very little reflection, mostly reaction, since I was the same way, I admired that in him. I also admired that he was successful in life using that, while I had been nothing but pretty much a failure. So after meeting someone like-mindedand enjoying it, we decided to stay in contact about things outside of concrete. We also agreed that his job looked poor and he should be credited some serious $$$ back You're damn right that to this day, at least until this comes out, no one in my company knew I had anything to do with him outside of work.I was all for it. Hey my life was sad, all I did was take care of my kids, pay child support and work. While there are others far worse off in life, I was absolutely miserable, I felt so empty inside, dead almost. Trying to keep up with the so called, "successful people," and failing, left me feeling hollow. Even in those moments when I did have moments of good fortune, it left me feeling hollow.

I remember calling him a few days later as I drove down 495 South with a notebook on my leg and pen in hand. We were bouncing ideas back and forth for names. We had worked up a combination list of about 50 so called "spiritual words." When I said the words, "Paranormal Spiritual Investigations," something clicked. He loved it, and we agreed to call ourselves that, PSI, (to this day, some so-called very spiritual people don't know that PSI stands for the latent psychic ability that we all possess). That was the start of our group, and every day we talked and every day we got each other pumped up about investigating haunted houses. What we would do, how it should be done, how famous we would become. It became a ray of sunshine in my day and when I was feeling depressed or frustrated, I could always count on a high energy conversation with him to pick me up. It was such a nice change from talking about, "this person sucks," or "guess how so and so screwed up this job?"all day with my co-workers or setting up play dates for my kids. It was so cool to connect with another human being on a deeper level for a change.

A few weeks later he called sounding somewhat depressed. He told me that there already was a group in our area called, "The Massachusetts Ghost Hunters."We spoke about them and the fact that they were doing an investigation in the famous Mansion in western MA. He told me it was open to the public and if you were willing to pay, anyone could go. It was an overnight trip and as I looked it up on the internet, I got more and more interested. Not only were there spooky tales about the mansion and tales of cobweb draped spirits tormenting people, butalso a variety of classes about spiritual abilities as well. It sounded like a great way to spend a weekend and we agreed to go, (also we could see and learn how the so called professionals investigated).

One of the classes being taught there was about protection from ghosts. It was something Tom and had spoken at length about. I mean it's exciting to go investigate a haunted house, but no one wants to potentially bring spirits home with them afterwards. After agreeing to go, and even being pumped about doing something involving the supernatural, my innate shittiness still almost made me cancel. Not only would it be an expense, but also I would have to find sitters for my kids and then pay them, so it would cost me double. My old self had a litany of woe and excuses, but Tom was a ball of energy and talked me into it in no time. As we discussed the itinerary, I shunted my doubts aside and agreed to go.

Even if you don't know anything about Massachusetts, a quick glance at a map will show you it's a really small state, so I was surprised to find out it was a three hour drive there. When we left in Tom's Humvee, he put a movie on for me and riding along in comfort and watching TV mollified me a lot. I guess there was something to this "luxury thing" after all.

Somewhere along the way he pulled out a .38, waved it around and told me he had one for me too if I wanted it. I am laughing as I type this, because I asked him, "What the hell man. You think we are going to shoot the spirits we encounter out there? Put that fricking thing away." To me, it should have been a warning sign, and part of me registered that it was. I came from the old school, and guns were no-no. If you had a beef, you solved them with your fists, but I ignored it and went back to the movie I was watching. We chatted away like magpies as we drove through the autumn hills of New England.

We arrived in the afternoon. As we drove up to the place, I thought to myself, "what a shithole." What a crappy building to be called a mansion, paint peeling, the missing window panes covered with cardboard, nothing really impressive about it. It didn't even have a proper parking lot, just a muddy yard that we drove into. I thought I would see some grand old house on a hilltop, a coupleof weeping willow trees hiding it, maybe someone in a white suit offering us mint juleps. It was really nothing like that at all. It was among other houses on the street, and looked like it belonged in the inner city somewhere. As we left the Humvee and climbed the stairs, I saw loose storm windows, a floor painted an ugly green shade and a oval rug that went out of style in the late 1950's. The furniture that looked like it came from the TV set of Archie Bunker. "Who the hell named this place?" I asked myself. As we walked in, I could see that it was built without purpose. The layout of the rooms didn't seem to make sense. One to the left, one to the right, a hallway opening into another room in front of you, hardly anything like the mansions I had seen in books and on TV. Where was the gold painted wainscoting? The chandelier made from the tusks of Eighteenth Century elephants? They sure as hell weren't there.

If this place was a mansion in western Mass, shit, Tom's house would have been a small kingdom out here. As I looked around and peered into the rooms near me, I saw that the one on the right was where people were selling items like crystals and feathers; someone was doing tarot card readings in the corner and on my left was a parlor decorated like the rest, poorly. Basically the mansion was this huge old house in various states of disrepair and if you were to Google it, you will quickly see what I mean. I expected to be greeted at the door and have to pay there, and then be led around on a guided tour by Peter Venkman, but it really was a kind of thing that was being winged.

We walked into this great big house and instead of reception and security guiding towards roped lines, it was just groups of people standing around talking. I was pretty disappointed in the first five minutes. Closer inspection showed me a small group of people standing around this scruffy looking guy with grey hair. He was a physically large person, a little overweight with a grey goatee shot with black hair, wearing a t-shirt with a picture of a wolf on it. As I walked up, I heard them talking about animals, and what they represented. Not knowing much of anything, I just hung back, quietly listening to their conversation. It seemed that each of us has an animal that we have a special affinity with, this is called an "animal totem," and it has lessons for us. Since I was late, we had just missed this class so I sidled up and inserted myself and said how sad I was that I had missed the class (hoping, hoping for him to say, "sure knucklehead, come on, I will show you. "a-ha. No such luck).

Beside the state of the so called mansion, it was pretty amazing to me. For the simple reason of everyone's open mindedness about ghosts. These people were talking about things that had been taboo for me, or something that only was brought up with my family or close friends. I loved that it didn't matter what I talked about, no matter how weird it was, there was someone who would understand it and be into it. I could have started talking about Atlanteans coming and mutilating our cattle while murdering Kennedy and someone would have been open to it. There were so many conversations, some about ghosts, yeti, UFOs and many about so-called, "energy." There were many hands shook and many, many introductions. Tom and I quickly split up and went our separate ways. I found myself sitting on the steps, smoking and talking with someone from the Western Mass Paranormal group and he said, "Yeah, I'm not really into this energy stuff," and I agreed. Hey, I am a concrete worker and I knew very little about energy, but given my experiences, I knew about ghosts. He and I sat there, smoking and speaking of things experienced and seen, I found myself happy. For the first time in a few years, I felt a level of contentment that sadly, I unaccustomed to. Here were people who knew and understood what I had been through and I could just sidle up to people and start talking about my experiencesand they would listen and nod. The more I talked to people, I could see that some were interested in me, (which was a total change from the usual "stop and get away from me whiny Norman") based on my stories and the things that I had experienced. It was great.

After walking around and introducing ourselves, we found that everyone was leaving to meet for dinner at a restaurant downtown. So we headed there to. There was a buffet dinner in which the Mass Ghost Hunters members would speak and since Tom and I showed up late, we sat at a table and started stuffing our faces.There were roughly about 50 people there and I distinctly remember Tom leaning over to me, pointing to a table of people and saying, "those are the Shamans, I talked with them earlier." Since he was so self-assured and confident, he stood up and he walked over to them, said something and everyone laughed. I find myself looking at him in amazement. He was the diametric opposite of me; successful, confident, so self-assured. I was lucky to be there with him, 38 or no 38. Surreptitiously checking out the Shamans while shoveling food down my throat, I saw that scruffy guy again and a few other ladies sitting with him. After dinner we went back to the Mansion for the night's activities.

These Shamans were important to me, because they later ended up becoming a large part of my life for some time. Initially, they were very standoffish and it was only Tom who had brought them close. I gotta hand it to the Massachusetts Ghost Hunters; they had this thing planned out pretty well. Even if the itinerary was winged, and they let groups of people stand around in the mansion, they did have some good activities for the night. There was some table tipping planned, (where people are mysteriously able to lift tables using one finger), Automatic writing, (blank paper, a pen and an empty mind), and finally a séance. I was really looking forward to the séance since I had read about them, but had never been to one before. So we attended and participated in all the activities. The table tipping was a little fake,(everyone sitting in a circle, four people each taking a side of a table, each only using one finger to lift it). It probably would've been good if the table was heavy, but in reality, two people with one finger could lift this thing and I could see people's fingers bending. With the automatic writing class, you weren't supposed to focus, just let your pen start writing and then after awhile, see what came out. Well, all I got was a sheet of paper full of scribbles. I guess that wasn't my area of expertise either. The séance was what changed my life. I can say now, my life was changed forever.

    We sat around this huge table. It wasn't exactly dark, but it wasn't bright either, just some candles softly glowing. I was separated from Tom and I remember the hosts and the Shamans gathering around and telling everyone they would keep space to protect us. Protect us from what? I don't know, but having seen, "The Exorcist, "and other scary movies, I knew I didn't want to be spewing green vomit out at the end of the night, so, keep the space! One of the hosts from Mass Ghost Hunters was sprinkling sea salt around the table in a circle on the floor. There was a lot of talking and laughing as it got down to business. I was sitting between two middle-aged women who were complete strangers, holding their hands. Do I need to speak of what a complete change of life direction this was for me? We all joined hands and were told to not to let go and to keep our eyes closed and our heads down. As I sat in that world of my own blackness,

I wasn't aware of anything. I just felt like a bit of jerk holding some strangers' hands, I heard movement near me and I knew it was one of the Shamans walking around, holding space, (whatever the hell that was). Then someone started speaking.

"Are there any spirits who would like to speak to us?"

Sure enough, someone asked, "Does anyone know anyone named John?"

"Yeah."

"Well, he wants you to know he's ok." A lot of bland stuff like that.

Tom said that "Archangel Michael wishes us to know he's with us."

Personally I didn't think that Tom had just channeled Archangel Michael, but hey, who was I to judge? I knew I wasn't getting told anything, at least wasn't hearing voices. Other than feeling that the ladies, whose hands I was holding, were running hot. I was just sitting there, while others were coming out with messages. All of a sudden I felt someone touch my upper thigh, (NOT THERE). It was so distinct, there was no doubting something had touched me. I actually peeked down to see if a ruler had fallen across my legs,(because that was what it had felt like, though there was no ruler on the table or near me, come to think of it, I doubt there was a ruler in the whole damn mansion) ,and then I got touched on my chest, again very clearly. It felt like someone standing in front of me just poked me with a finger, but the thing was, I knew no one was there.

The whole time I am freaking out about being touched, people are continuing to ask, "Anyone know a John

Smith?""Yes.""He's ok." Though I mock it, there was a few, "Did anyone know a Eunice?""Yes.""Did she have a problem with her heart?""Yes.""She says she's around you a lot." So it wasn't all junk, but what the hell did I care? I was getting felt up by the spirit world. Then a voice from behind me asked, "Does anyone have Native American blood in them here?"There had been talks and rumors about my ancestor's sluttiness, the Shaw side had agreed we had some Indian ancestors. "Yes," I said, (Well, what the hell, no one else was speaking up).He said, "There's someone here with a message for you."Then he proceeded to tell me about how the earth remembered the herds of deer and the endless fields of buffalo, the timeswhen the skies had darkened with the birds. The cool thing was, this was something my brother and I had discussed previously on multiple occasions. We had always speculated what it would be like to see the land before we humans had ruined it, before man was here. When Cape Cod, was named after the fact there was so much Cod there, and you didn't have to go 30 miles offshore to maybe catch one. Anyway, this really meant a lot to me, because it was something I often thought about. As I was marveling at this, I remember hearing someone starting to breathe really heavy, like starting to pant, and then they started to moan.

    Let me tell you something. Holding hands in the dark with strange women, listening to someone moan is kind of freaky. At first I didn't pay it too much attention because I was focused on the message I had just heard, but it registered in the back of my mind, and then someonesaid, "Paul's been jumped." What the hell ' being jumped' was, I didn't know, but I put my head down and kept holding hands like I had been instructed. I think to this day Paul denies it, but all 50 of us who were there, we know what happened. The breathing got more labored and Paul started moaning as well. I was just sitting there with my head down listening to this for about 20 seconds when someone said, "Say the lord's prayer," and all 50 of us joined into one voice and said the Lord's Prayer.

My command of the English tongue fails me here. I cannot correctly communicate what happened in that moment. Please bear with me, as I try.

Here I was, this miserable person, holding hands with two strangers, feeling things, getting touched. I am sitting in the dark, some guy is moaning and we all start saying the Lord's Prayer. You know how in the bible in the book of Exodus, there's the passage where it says, "and God hardened Pharaoh's heart?" That's what I had allowed to happen to me. My heart had been hardened. I thought for the most part that everyone sucked. "Get out of my fucking way!" was my usual thought as I sped maliciously through life. My heart was hardened. I mean, I loved my kids, but I would find myself staring at people in front of me at the line at the grocery store, wishing they would move or didn't exist at all. Angry driver? Ha ha. I was the ultimate road rage guy, fist pounding on the dash, get out of my way!!!!! Well, when we started saying the Lord's Prayer, in that moment it was like God touched my heart. ←That sentence sucks compared to what I felt. But in one perfect moment in my life, God touched me, and as I sat there and held everyone's hands I wanted to shout and sing,"Ahhhhhhhhhhhhhhhahhhahhhhhhahhhhhhhhha" or hosannas or anything that expressed what I felt. Because in that one second I remembered what was important in life, and it wasn't going out or getting laid, or getting ahead and selling a million feet of concrete decking and getting rich. In that one moment I remembered why I was here and for what purpose. When that God finger touched my heart, I remembered love, not conditional love that relies upon getting what we want, no this was the love that I felt when I first saw my children born. It felt so good. It was the simplest most basic thing. It was and is, the complete opposite of stress and frustration. It was joy, joy to be alive, joy to care for the other person, satisfaction, endless patience, understanding; it was love, as simple as that. As we all grow old, that love that we feel all the time as kids becomes hardened and lost and eventually forgotten. In that moment I remembered love, and I will spend the rest of my days thanking God for that blessing. I know it sounds corny, but it's true. In that moment, I realized everything I had experienced and suffered was shit, and guess what? It didn't matter, because I felt love. All my complaints, all my worry, were nothing, love. Search your heart and try to remember the last time you looked at something or someone perfectly and without expectation. Try and remember when you truly cared about someone more than yourself. If you can think of something right off of top of your head, thank God, because you are lucky.

Since that day I have studied much esoteric knowledge. One thing that comes close is a state of mind called, "Samadhi." Samadhi is usually described as oneness with God. A kind of super consciousness that a Yogi, after many years of training, reaches. There, the Yogi is able to meditate and be one with God/Allah/Creator/Odin, whatever you want to call him/her. The Yogi is also able to bring their students to this state for a brief period of time. Then because of their many impurities, they cannot maintain it. Well, this is what that sounds like. It felt like unconditional love, a river of it, a vast ocean of love deeper than my mind could perceive, and enough to heal me of 10 years of self pity in an instant.

For me, it was mind blowing. To this day, I don't remember what happened after, only that when I opened my eyes I looked right down at the floor to see if something was laying there from touching me. There was nothing. I looked for a ruler, nothing, a stick, a branch, a pencil, anything that would explain why I was being poked. I slowly let go of the ladies' hands, smiled at them and looked around. A bunch of people were standing around Paul, but I was feeling my heart and wondering. Everything I just said pales in comparison to what I felt, but it's the best I can do. The grin had returned to my face. Tom came over and we were both excited, him about channeling Archangel Michael, (insert raised eyebrow here), and I about being hit on by the spirit world, and getting my message. I couldn't tell him about the heart, or maybe I did, I forget it all in the memory of that moment. Anyway, that wrapped up the night. We had gotten a hotel room close by, so Tom and I went back and laid there for awhile comparingstories and experiences. We talked about Paul and what had happened, the different messages people had gotten. The whole time, as I am lying there talking about ghosts and séances, my mind is thinking about that moment, that perfect fucking moment, when I remembered.

    The next morning, we showed up ready to learn. A woman there, Susan, was teaching classes on how to protect yourself from the spirit world. It was basically all these different things you can do; picture white light, take sea salt baths,etc, simple things really. She spoke for some time about Cords and cutting Cords??? What the hell are Cords? Well, listening and talking afterwards to Susan, I learned that as people, we often attach to each other energetically and remain connected. This is why you will keep thinking of someone for hours or days after you've argued with them. She also spoke about grounding. This was a form of meditation to help focus and feel calmer. Since this was something I knew I needed, I paid attention and took notes which I think I still have somewhere. While I didn't know much about this energy stuff people kept talking about, I was an eager student, especially after the night before. After her presentation was over, we talked with her at length and got her interested in PSI and what we were doing. She was from our neck of the woods and she mentioned how she was trying to overcome her fear of the spirit world and she thought it would help her to go on investigations with us. She knew a hell of a lot more than I did, and more importantly, to me, she was very cute. After leaving her we met with the Shamans again and I got smudged for the first time. It was where someone with a feather and a shell filled with burning sage, brushed smoke all over you. This was supposed to remove spirits from your energy field. Since I knew I had lived in haunted houses for most of my life, smudge away baby! The funny thing was, I got a ton of chills, the kind that make you say things like, "blat," and "plurp."After saying, "plurk," and shaking with the force of it, the shaman laughed and explained it as a spirit leaving my energy field. Whoa. Well, I shuddered ten times. I guess I had a lot of ghosts hitchhiking,(which didn't surprise me). After being smudged, we talked with the Shamanic people for a couple of hours, learning from them about their beliefs in the spirit world. They really had some exotic theories, some of which made me raise an inner eyebrow. Yet on some level a lot of what they said made sense to me, especially given all I had experienced. They told us how spirits can attach to you and feed from like energy.

Let me give you an example. Since everything is energy and we all have these energy fields around us, everything you do and believe shows in your energy field. Now, I love smoking. Man, nothing beats a smoke. Well, if I die and am stuck on the other side, I can't smoke anymore, so what's the next best thing? Hanging around someone that smokes telling them, "have another butt, have a smoke," because I can feed from the energy of it. Now you take every human addiction and emotion that way, and you see how dysfunctions can spiral out of control. Think about that for a moment. Usually our addictions get worse and worse. Now I am not explaining away any human behavior, ultimately I choose to smoke, but it certainly makes it harder to stop when someone is whispering in your ear all day.

I also heard people talk about chakras and since Tom acted like he knew what a chakra was, I pretended I did too. I remember the scruffy looking Shaman, putting his hand on my chest and asking me if I "felt that." Since I didn't want to sound like the only one there who didn't, my reply was, "Wow, hell ya!" He told me he was opening my heart chakra. Well, I didn't know anything about that, but I knew after feeling Gods love, I was open to learning and I listened. To me, even just the brief talks we had had, the Shaman's theories explained some of mysteries in my life. The presence I had always felt, why I had always lived in haunted houses and such. Some of what they said really resonated with me. While I was talking to them, Tom was pretty quickly putting the moves on a very attractive lady Shaman. It was through that, that we were formally introduced to them, for some reason, they were all blonde of one shade or another. Talking, we also found out they were from our area and more importantly there was a place close to us that everyone met on Monday nights to get together and learn. Their casual, "You should come to healing circle," was met with eagerness and we agreed to go the following week.

We headed home soon after. I had to get my kids and it was a long drive back and basically everything we were interested in, was for the most part, done. It was silent ride home. Tom and I talked a little about what we had seen, but we were both lost in our own worlds. I watched a movie as he drove,(God I wish I was rich), mostly lost in my mind, thinking of what I had felt. When I got my kids, we went food shopping and I remember them asking me, "Dad, why are you so quiet?" I really was soft spoken for a couple of days after, (people at work kept asking me to speak up).It wasn't until much later that I read that deep healings often do that to people. Well, I was deeply healed.

CHAPTER 8

So I was healed, and my life changed for the better in every way. Butterflies would land on my brow while bluebirds circled my head. Far from it. I still had to live in the real world and work, but I was different. I felt different. I felt calm. That inner demon that had tormented me, made me worry and stress out, was quiet all of a sudden. I felt so peaceful inside, remembering that love, that, "poor me, why me" dude had been told to shut up, and he did, because even he was humbled by what I felt. I could see the purpose of everything I had been through. Why I had to get divorced and all the stress; it was to bring me to this point. It was like someone was standing next to me saying, "We are glad you are here finally." Reality is, someone probably was.

The healing, not only had it opened that hardened heart, but it showed me reason to slow down and enjoy. Think of it this way. I woke up at 4:30 a.m., drove 80 MPH to work so I could get there before 6:00 a.m. and get yelled at. Then I drove 80MPH to the job site to work as hard as I could to finish as quickly as I could, because I had to drive 80 MPH to a sales appointment or another job, to work as hard as I could, to drive 80 MPH home, to get my kids and take care of them. I would get my children, make dinner, take them to the park, go to the store, go home, get them ready for bed and then relax on the computer or in front of the TV and go to bed at 11:00 p.m. or so. I am tired just writing this, I bet you're tired just reading this. My whole life was high speed and part of the healing showed me that it was nonsense. If I took five minutes out of my insane day to relax and appreciate the beauty around me, what the hell is five minutes going to matter? Not one bit. More and more I realized all the things that had frustrated me, were my own fault. I couldn't lay the blame on anyone but myself and all the bitching and whining I had done over the last six years, it didn't change anything, all it did was make me a whiny bitch. All I was really doing was complaining about myself.

After years of being closed off and only somewhat friendly to friends and co-workers, I was meeting new people and learning about energy and the spirit world. I knew about ghosts but everyone talked about this mysterious "energy," how it was used and what we could do with it. Through conversations with Tom and Susan, I was soon learning at a geometric rate. I had heard of Kirellian photographs and knew all the lingo, "good vibes, bad energy, far out man !" Well here was conversation after conversation about energy, how it was used, what it did, etc, etc. I learned so much in such a short time about energy work that it was almost like I was meant too.

Of course I was.

It was explained in the simplest of terms to me. Ponder for a moment how someone can be angry in the same room with you. They don't have to say a single word, yet you know it.

Energy. Think of how someone pops into your head and then they call you, energy. How about some people make you tired, energy? To Tom and Susan, everything was energy. Since they were to me, wonderful open people, I paid attention to what they said. They told me how we all have these energy fields and when you argue with someone, you both connect energetically, it's called, "Cording." It made sense, because as a parent, I knew when my kids were in trouble or feeling crappy =Cords. How many times have you had a confrontation with someone and they get stuck in your head, your thoughts keep returning to them? Cords. I used to be heavily corded to people because I was sensitive and open, so it was easy for people to connect to me. So we all have this energy swirling around us, all the time. Everything we think, believe, know, eat, crap, everything, shows up in this field. That's how people keep attracting things. That's how I kept attracting spirits. Because they could see in my energy field that I was sensitive to them, (and as scared as hell).

Is this so hard to believe? Well, then I ask you this. In every town in America, almost every small town, every city, there are acupuncturists. What is acupuncture? It is the belief that we have energy that flows through our body and there are certain junctures where it collects like eddies in the stream, called meridians. Get a blockage in one of those eddies and you get fat, or have back pain, etc.Acupuncturists believe that by poking it with needles you can get the energy flowing again. Studies have shown that many acupuncture points have a dramatically decreased electrical resistance compared with points on the skin surrounding it (10 Kilo-ohms at the center of a point, compared to 3 mega-ohms in the surrounding skin) **"The Field" Lynn McTaggart PG 55.** What does that mean? It means that science has shown that there is some variation in our bodies that correspond with ancient knowledge relating to the bodies energy field. The validity of which is well documented by the American Medical Association.

Back to our story.

It was about two weeks after the Mansion that I realized I needed to start meditating. I remember driving in the fast lane with my knee, eating a cheeseburger, smoking a cigarette and talking on the phone. All of a sudden I looked at myself and what I was doing, and pitched everything right out the window. I slowed down and sat there thinking. I knew I had to start meditating, I knew it, it was an urge, a need to begin to slow my mind down or to take a moment and just do nothing. How? I've always tried to be self sufficient in a lot of ways and something guided me to be this way in meditation. So one night after I put the kids to bed, I sat on my couch and closed my eyes and started trying not to think. Ha ha, have you ever tried not to think? Good luck with that American! Your whole here life has taught you to multitask. Come on, you can walk and chew gum, you can drive and talk on the phone, you can do this while doing that. This 80MPH life I had been leading for eight or so years made that impossible. I think I sat there for what seemed likeeight hours and when I opened my eyes four minutes had gone past.

The next night I tried chanting the same word over and over again, thinking that this would be different. After saying it about 40,000 times, I opened my eyes and saw that ten minutes had passed.

Great.

One word I had kept hearing from my new friends was, "Chakra." Now, I didn't know what a chakra was, but I didn't tell anyone that. I just nodded my head and stroked my goatee when conversation turned to them.

So I went online and read a little. What I learned was that this mysterious energy my friends kept talking about was powered by our Chakras. Think of it as this great big egg surrounding your body, reaching out in every direction. That's your energy field, your aura. Now, inside it are these balls of energy, each with a different location on the body, each relating to a different set of emotions. For example, your heart chakra relates to love and compassion, for yourself and others. Well tell me, how do most business men die? Heart attacks, why? Well, either they don't care for other people or aren't very compassionate and as such they start to close off their heart chakra. And before Forbes brings lawsuits against me, yes, I am making a broad statement to support my idea, either accept or don't, it doesn't matter that much to me.

So we have energy fields around our bodies, and what I learned from Google was that they are powered by these centers called Chakras. These Chakras relate to different emotions, different parts of our bodies. When I was realized I needed to meditate, I decided to meditate on my chakras after finding where they were located. I wanted to try and feel them, so I started thinking about how I should just sit there and meditate and picture them opening. That was my meditation. I sat and opened my Chakras and would picture the colors and try to feel the location of where I had read they should be. And you know what? It worked. The first time I tried it, I opened my eyes and 40 minutes had passed. To those doubters, sit there and try to do nothing but visualize something for 40 minutes. Now do it every night for a month. Try it, its hard. I had learned to meditate.

Following what we had learned at the ghost hunt and from talking to the Shamans, we learned there was a metaphysical place only a few towns over from us called, "Angels Sanctuary." Tom and I started going there on Monday nights. (Monday and Tuesday nights were when I didn't have my children.) I remember thinking that this place would be glowing white and shiny, maybe some angels floating around, or maybe it would be a giant Teepee we could all sit in. Well, when we got there, it was a house, a nice one, much nicer than the Mansion, but still just a house. As I walked up, I saw smokers outside chuffing away on cigarettes. Seeing spiritual people smoking made me happy for some reason. Tom went in and I stayed out and had a smoke along with them. I made some small talk and then headed inside. I found Tom chatting with some of the women we had met at the Mansion. There was a lot of hugging and smiles and then we were told we were going to begin.

I could almost write a book on just the next two years of my life alone, all the training and learning that I went through. I learned lifetimes of energy work in such a short time. I will gloss over it, and just illuminate a few key things that happened.

My co-workers were still unawareanything was different, since we had limited contact. I was still working like a jerk and goofing around, but less and less often did I show up to the job complaining about people and things. Less and less would I let frustrations stress me out,(and think about concrete for a moment, you have 3 hours to do your job perfectly, if something goes wrong, you have a $10,000 mistake on your hands that needs to be painfully removed with jackhammers). Soon, I found nothing related to work could cause me to worry. What's your job compared to how you feel about your kids? Nothing. I could pour the pyramid, or make the most amazing tabletops and in 200 years, no one would know a fucking thing about me. I realized my legacy was how those around me felt about me now, the memory of me that they would carry forward. Every day I would talk on the phone and learn, or think of things and feel and ask someone. Tom and I continued to go to Angels Sanctuary on

Mondays to meditate and talk to everyone there. Every time we showed up, people would hug me and let me know they were glad I had come. I remember the first time a man said, "Give me a hug," and opened his arms. Part of me rebelled,(two men hugging? Wtf ?), but then I knew it wasn't because he was attracted to me. It was that he felt love and wanted to show it and I hugged him back. Or even holding hands, running energy, ha-ha, imagine a concrete worker standing in a circle holding hands with men, and being comfortable with it? After a few times, I stopped being self conscious, and I would hold someone's hand with a smile.

     One Monday we showed up and instead of meditation they were having a movie night. A few people used it as an excuse to leave and do some errands, but a couple who had driven some distance didn't want to go home early. So after a little discussion and some hemming and hawing a couple Shamans and I decided to check out a local cemetery. We followed each other in our vehicles and met in the parking lot across the street from the cemetery in Chelmsford Center. It was old, with tombstones leaning crazily like bad broken teeth. Usually one cemetery is like any other except that this one is a rolling expanse and climbs about 100 feet to a hilltop. It's surrounded by houses, so we were pretty quiet as we walked around.

     OK, don't ask. Don't ask what the hell we were doing in a cemetery at 8:00 p.m. on an early fall night. All I knew was that I was cranking in the high vibe with my friends and I didn't really want to go home. We walked in and started heading towards the top. I actually saw something white about three feet tall, run from one tombstone to another to another, right in front of me. My friend pointed right at it and said, "Did you see that?" When we walked over there, there was nothing. We both had seen something that disappeared. After some whispered, excited conversation, we continued on. When we got to the top of the hill, we walked into a distinct cold spot. The Shamans told me, "there's something here that doesn't like us," and we made a circle and held hands and started running energy between us.

That's what it was and what we did. We joined hands, and felt energy running between us. If you can imagine that we are all batteries, (We are you know. We eat food and convert it into electricity that we use to power our muscles.) I'm a 9 volt, you're a 9 volt and so is everyone else; well, when you combine three 9 volts, you don't get 27 volts, you get perhaps 50 volts, something more powerful than the one. I always heard people say, "Open your hahhht," and eventually I came to understand that it wasn't so much picturing blood spewing out of my chest as it was visualizing the color associated with your heart chakra brightening. So when in doubt or trying to do something, we would join hands and run energy and raise our vibrations. That's what we did there. We all felt a huge cold spot and we joined hands and pictured our hearts opening, (understand, crappy spirits don't like love, that's the opposite of them).So I am standing there, on a cool fall evening in a cemetery in Chelmsford MA, holding hands with two of my friends, imagining, visualizing my heart opening and then I actually feel something like a hand come in and squeeze my heart. Imagine that for a second. Imagine feeling a cold spot come and squeeze your heart, to the point that it physically hurts. It made me wince and pause for a moment and then I just laughed, visualizing my heart opening even wider. I mean come on, I had felt love, pure love and nothing stupid was going to scare me. It went away, and as I closed my eyes, all of sudden I saw an image of an old farmer, just seeing the mental picture in your head. I told them, and we stood there in the cemetery on a September night and shared what we were seeing in our minds.

That's how a lot of people do it you know; mediums, psychics. They get shown an image and they trust it implicitly. Since spirits project emotion, pictures, they get shown, and they follow it, and then they get shown something else and so on and so on. We stayed there and exchanged what we saw back and forth. We said a prayer and about ten minutes later we ended up leaving. Personally, it was my first experience with the spirit world that didn't end up with me being afraid and/or running for my life. When I think about it now, I was grateful I had company to help keep that hand from my heart. More importantly, it was good to have what I sensed confirmed by others.

CHAPTER 9

It was the middle of October when Tom called me, excited. It seems his wife, who was a hairdresser, had a friend that was going through a tough time. Her husband had endured a string of bad luck and recently she and her kids had been experiencing things a bit out of the normal realm, culminating in hundreds of crows landing in their yard. From the way he described it, the whole neighborhood had gathered around to witness that black, obnoxious carpet cawing away on their lawn. As he told me what they were going through, especially the oldest daughter had experienced, I couldn't help but think poltergeist. He was all pumped and got me excited as PSI was going on its first investigation. We spoke to Susan and she agreed to go as well.

We met the following night in Georgetown around 5:30 p.m. Since Georgetown is right next to my work, I met them at the house. As we climbed out of our vehicles, I marveled at this beautiful fall evening, it was spring weather, a balmy 60. I walked down the driveway with them, talking and laughing.

Hoping to at least make some sense of whatever was happening to these people. I saw the house was a cute little gray Cape Cod, with black shutters. I looked around the yard and didn't see a single crow, which in a way was a relief because I still didn't know how I felt about that yet. Even before we had knocked, Tom was doing crazy stuff. He walked up to the front door and did a geometric intention on it. It was something we had seen some of the Shamans at Angels Sanctuary do and I think he wanted to be like them. I raised an eyebrow, but kept quiet. The moment after he did this, the door opened and I saw a lovely young mom with a toddler held on her hip. Everyone exchanged greetings as Susan pulled out a smudge stick the size of a large submarine sandwich. Since I was the scientific one, I was introduced to the husband and the daughter first and interviewed them. I sat at the kitchen table and started doing what I do best, which is talking. Tom and Susan went off to explore the house with the wife, as I sat there and listened to the husband tell me of the last five years of his life. I sat at the table, looking at his softly yellowing skin, dark hair and bloodshot eyes and I felt bad. It was actually quite sad, and in a lot of ways I could relate to the horror story of bad luck he was telling me. But I didn't feel a lot of sympathy as he sat there bleary eyed, swigging down canned beer while two little boys ran around yelling. We talked for awhile and I took notes while he drank away a case of beer. He had some serious issues with his ex-wife, and thought the whole cause of his bad luck was from her. He told me she was into black magic, how she was angry with him. You get the point. Anyway, after we were through talking, I went out for a smoke on the back porch and asked the daughter to follow me so I could speak with her. I wanted to get her away from step-dad, whom even in my relatively oblivious state, I could feel animosity radiating from her, towards him. Since most poltergeists tend to center around a young teenager, I was hoping that she was the key. I stood out on the back deck and smoked, talking to this young girl, trying to get her to open up to a stranger she had just met. She had dirty blonde hair and the blooming acne problem that I remember from my own youth. After talking about mundane stuff for a bit, she told me a few different things that had happened. She had seen the phone flash 666, doors opening by themselves, things moving. The sort of traditional haunting that we have come to expect. I was interested in her relationship with her step dad.

I had learned that most poltergeists usually involve a teenager going through some emotional turmoil. Whether it's the hormones combined with angst, or vice versa, once you remove the teen, poltergeists tend to settle down. Now I know that it's a spirit that uses a teen's energy to manipulate matter. Think of how much you feel and go through as a teen, all those emotions are crazy and you're leaking energy like the titanic after the iceberg. Anyway, after two smokes I was done talking to her and I went in to talk to the mom. Before I did, Tom and Susan took me on a tour of the house. They showed me a couple rooms where they had sensed different energies. Tom pointed out a bookcase where some black magic books were hidden, raising an eyebrow, he gave me an,"ah ha," nod.

I think it was about 6:30p.m when I sat on the living room couch with the wife. Her sons were running around, yelling, just being kids. Since this was her house and she was the matron, at first it was hard to get her attention from the children who were using the opportunity of moms distraction to cause mischief. Once I got her focused on me, she started telling me how a month prior she had woken up in the middle of the night. Her heart was racing and she could feel energy rushing up and down her body. She said that she actually thought she was going to die and made out a will for her husband and wrote a note saying goodbye to her kids. She told me she had been feeling weird since then and her hands had been freezing every day. "Until Tom did that thing," which I took to mean smudging her, she said she now felt better. I started talkingabout details, taking notes and asking about what she had experienced. Then she said, "You know, sitting here next to you, I am starting to feel cold again."

Great, I always knew I had a way with women.

I stood up, "Well let me get Tom and Susan, and they can make you right again." I went back into the kitchen and sat at the table as they went back into the living room with the wife. I started making small talk with the dad, and he called the kids into the kitchen. We heard murmuring coming from the other room, a lot of murmuring. I poked my head around the corner and saw Susan holding the woman's feet, and Tom holding her hands. I stare for a moment and decide I pretty much know nothing so I head back into the kitchen.

I go out for a smoke, come in, and hear chanting coming from the other room, honestly, it was like something you would expect to hear from a temple. I looked in and Susan is holding this woman's ankles and rocking back and forth and chanting, "ommmmm." I don't know how long I stood there with my mouth agape, but all of a sudden I realizedthat the kids and the husband were standing next to me, doing the same thing. So I collect myself and sit back down and ask the kids to draw pictures for me. For a while that was my job, to try and keep the kids out of the room, distract them, ease the dad's rolling eyes. To try distract them from the chanting and whatever is going on with his wife. Remember I was the scientific one, what did I know about energy or anything? So I am sitting there, in Georgetown, Massachusetts, its around 7 at night after a long day of supervising concrete workers, and there's this housewife with a place full of kids with one of my friends holding her feet chanting, "ommmmmmmmmmmm" over and over. I seriously stopped and thought, "what did I get myself into?"

That's when I started hearing the woman moan, like someone in the midst of an illness in a deep sleep, a restless kind of moan that speaks of bad dreams and sour, rotted fruit. I peek around the corner after telling the kids to go to dad, and I see her head slowly thrashing from side to side. "Whoa," I say softly to myself, "what the fuck is going on in there?" From coming here to investigate a supposed case of black magic and poltergeists, something is going down that looks like a bad dream. I sit back down and start making small talk with the father, talking to the kids, basically trying to distract everyone, when Tom says, "Norman, we need your help in here." I get up and walk into the room and see the lady is in a bad state. Susan is kneeling in front of her, still holding her ankles, and Tom is standing behind Susan with his hands on her shoulders. On a rudimentary level I know what he's doing, he's trying to run energy into Susan. I walk up behind Tom and place my hands on his back. I'm trying to imagine energy running from me, into him. It's the only thing I can think to do, other than run screaming from the house and going to find a catholic priest. So as I stand there, running energy into Tom, who's running energy into Susan, (Laurel and Hardy anyone?), an image pops into my head and I picture all of the energy in the room, being pulled into me. So I do that, and clear as day I see myself, (mentally imagine), walk over, place a hand on her forehead and yell, "Be gone."

Do I do it? No, I am here working with a medium and a professional psychic, what the hell do I know?

I hesitate for a moment and whisper, "Be gone," and Tom copies me. She ignores us, thrashing and moaning, I know whatever it was, didn't work. So I continue to run energy into Tom and the lady continues to suffer and moan. Tom stops and goes over and sits next to her on the couch and asks the family, (which is peeking around the corner at us, with eyes the size of saucers), to give him a glass of water. He gets it, I go and stand behind Susan and place my hands on her shoulders to run energy into her. Tom puts the glass to her hands and says, "You're ok, you're ok, take a drink, have some water." I then noticed that her fingers are as twisted and palsied as an old arthritic woman's. Seriously, her hands are like claws, she cannot even grip the glass and he has to hold it for her as she takes a couple of sips. "You're ok, you're ok, come back to us," he says and starts putting his hands over her chakra's, running energy on her. The husband peeks in, sees Tom's hand over his wife's chest, raises an eyebrow and herds the kids out again. I am standing behind Susan as I watch this. The woman starts moaning and thrashing again, saying over and over, "I'm cold, I'm so cold."

To say that I am not feeling the greatest about this, well, it's a serious fucking understatement. Here we were trying to start a group and the subject of our first investigation was sitting there moaning on the couch like a zombie. I stared at this woman thrashing about saying she was cold, all I felt was sympathy and compassion. I went over and kneeled before her, and took her hands in mine, "Feel my hands, see how warm they are."

"I can't feel anything." She was starting to cry now, "I can't feel hate, or anger, I can't feel my legs or my hands."

I looked at her. "That's exactly the opposite of what you need to feel right now, you need to feel love."

I took her claws more in mine, and I motioned to her daughter who was watching. "Remember when your daughter was born, and you first held her, remember how you felt?

Remember that little hunk of baloney in your hands who had never done anything besides make you want to pee? Remember how you held her, and all you felt was love?" Her eyes met mine for the first time since she sat on the couch. "And your husband, remember when you looked at him and realized he was the man you wanted to spend the rest of your life with, that you wanted to grow old with." I paused and took a breath, "and your first son, remember how proud you were when you saw him. A son! He had never done anything, and yet you loved him with all your heart." She actually started laughing, as I held onto her hands, and then noticed that she was crying and I was crying as well. We were both crying like a couple of babies and laughing together about it. Maybe in part because of what was happening, but more in part cause I was remembering the beauty and love of children entering the world. I was feeling the love that I felt when my kids entered the world, the love of a lifetime and the love that God had allowed me to feel again in the Mansion. She sat up. "I had to laugh because when my son was born, it hurt so much, I didn't want my daughter getting scared since she was in the room with me, so every time it hurt I laughed." She looked around at us, as Susan released her feet. "I feel much better now thank you," and she took Tom's offered glass of water and sat up straight.

Freaky shit, let me tell you.

The rest was anticlimactic. Tom promised to come back with the Shamanic people and clear the place for good the following week. We gathered our things and quietly left, with many hugs from the wife, and uncomprehending stares and handshakes from the husband. As we walked down the driveway, Tom kept saying how cool it was. They both kept mentioning, "Did you hear her talking about how she couldn't feel hate? Or anger? What kind of issues does she have?" They didn't get the idea of possession. When we reached our vehicles, we held hands and recited the Lord's Prayer, (we were assured if you had a demon with you, you couldn't say it without making a mistake) ,and called it a night.

Now let me say something about possession. There are evil spirits out there and some of them do want to possess people. What they do is they feed from an addiction or dysfunction the host possesses. If you know someone addicted to cocaine, you can be damn sure they've got something around them. Whispering, "do more, do some coke," etc., etc, so it can feed from the energy of it. So a spirit gets into their energy field, to the possessed individual, and it would feel like being cold or something alien and foreign to themselves, coming over them. Even in the summer, they would be shaking like they were freezing to death. (Remember the woman's story, how she felt cold.) I know. It's happened to me. You feel cold, almost like the chill of death, and get scared. That is exactly what it wants. It wants you afraid, wondering who this thing is inside you, what's going on, are you going to die?? You get frightened, it gets in deeper, more afraid, more deeper, till the mind snaps. Or you're like me, you got something hanging around you, whispering and tormenting you for years. Possession is real, and I've seen it happen a few times in all its aspects (beginning, possessed and afterwards). Again, let me thank God for the healing he did on me in the Mansion, and thank creator for letting me be able to help this woman.

CHAPTER 10

So needless to say, I don't think I slept too well. The next morning Tom had me on the phone telling me how cool he thought last night was, what we did. I really thought he was a moron with no idea what he was talking about.

I had talked to a Shaman on the ride home telling her about it, telling her about Tom opening up intentions with no concept of the consequences. She agreed and stroked my ego and helped calm me down some. Later on, someone else we both knew called and was shocked when I told her what happened and I told her how stupid I thought Tom was. I was really aggravated. We had gone to that house to help someone and ended up with an "almost" case of full-blown possession. WTF? Tom and I argued often through the day, and to sum it up, while I was driving through Douglas, Mass. for work, he told me I was just scared. Man, did that piss me off. I wasn't the one saying, "you're ok, you're ok," while my hand shook, holding a glass of water. I told him, "At no point was I scared Tom, I was concerned for the client, but that's it. What the hell did we do there last night? Almost get a woman possessed? How is that cool?" Needless to say, it got worse from there.

 A couple of days later it was Halloween. After taking my children out trick or treating, I had asked Tom and a Shaman to meet me down Coggers. I thought that it would be a perfect Halloween treat for spiritual people. I mean hang out in the haunted woods? Sure, it's Halloween, let's do it! Well, they blew me off. The friend canceled, and once she did, Tom did too. He told me, "You're not stepping foot in my house if you go down there!" I laughed because I was done listening to him. He had shown me what he thought spirituality was and moreover, he was afraid. I wasn't, I knew the secret, I had love in my heart and I was never going to be afraid again.

 I walked down to the edge of the pond. It was a nice quiet night, the stars were out. I remember I was in a light coat, and for an October night, I couldn't even see my breath. I stood there on the shoreline, looking across at all the new construction, remembering the woods I had loved. What they looked like and all the good times we had had down there. I felt assured of the perfection of my life, of all lives, and I started opening my chakras as I do when I meditate. I stood there and slowly opened them one by one. All of a sudden from nowhere a freight train of wind came blowing from across the pond. I thought to myself, "Fuck, it's here," and I turned and ran up the hill, reverting back to that scared child. When I got to the top of the hill and saw street lights and houses, I calmed down a bit. The wind continued to blow, but not directly at me as I had thought, it was diffused by the trees. I walked down the street in front of my parents' house and called Tom. I don't remember exactly what we talked about, except that I tried to get him to come over. He wouldn't and while I was talking to him, I noticed I kept hearing ticks and baps coming from things near me. They came from everywhere, my mom's car, the fence, the neighbor's car, nothing loud and obnoxious, but enough in my heightened sense that I noticed it. More importantly, after getting off the phone with Tom, I remembered that I had love in my heart and nothing to fear. Ever. I walked back down to Cogs and to the top of the hill, and I stood there and opened my energy field and my chakras. I can't describe what I felt standing there, just that I knew I wasn't alone. I remember activating the recorder on my phone and seeing if I could get someone's voice, I had no doubt there were spirits all around me. Then all of a sudden, as I stood there on Halloween night and opened my energy field, I felt a woman standing behind me to the left, in the trees. I knew she was there, and when I turned around to look, I thought for sure I would see her. I stood there for a few more minutes and finished my meditation. I had what we call, "a knowing." How many times have you just known something was wrong, or right? Or that someone you loved was in trouble? Well, this was just like that, except that it involved "knowing" a spirit was present. As I walked down the hill, all of sudden I thought, "They cut her fucking head off after they raped her!" I stopped dead in my tracks and looked over to where I knew she was standing. "I will be back with some friends, we will help you." I said this out loud to the trees, and then continued on my way. When I got in my truck and turned around at the end of the street, I thought for sure I was going to see her standing there. There wasn't a doubt in my mind that there was a woman there.

  A few days later I got a call from Tom telling me that he thought everything the Shamans were doing was evil. Playing with the spirit world was evil, ghosts were evil, and crystals were evil. Telling me that energy work was evil and basically telling me, that as long as I continued to do what I did, I was evil in his eyes too. I tried to convince him otherwise, and we had many long and painful conversations about it.

Every day he would call me and try to convince me to join him in church. I heard that since I used crystals to focus energy, that I was worshipping them. That the Shamans only got spirits to attach to us, so that they could get rid of them and look good. He had a litany of bad luck that had happened to him since he had started doing this spirituality stuff. What struck me as weird was he kept complaining about his electronics, telling me how his phones would die, his new TV died, followed by, "this never happens to me, ever." I remember one line in particular, "Norman this is me! This stuff doesn't happen to me, I always have great luck!"

Ha ha, basically, he reminded me of the old me.

All the arguing about religion and about God, (and trust me, we argued), all they did was serve to reinforce my beliefs. They only made me trust more and believe more in what I knew was right. He would fight with me, and I would have to defend what I thought, and in doing so, I reaffirmed what I had been shown, what I had learned. I am so glad that it had happened that way, because it served to strengthen my faith in God, in my own manner. To me, it didn't matter what you did, what you thought or believed, just that you made your own peace with life.

Don't you think that's missing from this world of medications? The simple ability to be content? As I've always told others, "I don't care if you worship frogs, just be happy and don't push it on me," and I kept trying to tell Tom that. I don't believe that if I am a good man, and try my best to help other people, I am doomed because I don't believe something. That doesn't make sense to me, and my arguments with Tom served to make me not only believe it, but to "Know" it.

One day I received a call and heard how he had thrown out all his books and all his crystals, since they were inherently evil. I went berserk! (I had given him two great books on the paranormal that cost me $30) and I told him so. Crystals? This guy had an awesome collection and I thought of all the money wasted and called him a moron. After hanging up, he called me back and said he had one box of them left, and I was welcome to it but, "to get them off my fucking property today!" Since my workday was taking me past his area, I swung by and threw the box in the back of my pickup. While I was on my way up to the job I was doing, my cell phone died. I restarted it, it died again. Then my work phone died. I raised an eyebrow and looked in the rearview mirror at the box of crystals sitting there, and I started to notice a pain in the left side of my neck. Great, but I ignored it and continued on. When I got to the job I was glad to get out of the truck and be away from those damn crystals even for just a little while. Driving back home, my neck was killing me. It got so bad that I almost pulled off the road, just to get out, run around, yell, rub my neck. I don't know. I wanted out of that truck and it took a lot of self-control not to leap from it, freaking out and yelling on the side of the highway about spirits and crystals. I began to think that Tom was right, maybe the Shamans did get spirits to attach to people so they could take them off, and look good. Maybe this was evil, maybe it wasn't, blah blah blah. My mind was racing a thousand miles an hour and all of my thoughts were shitty. It was the exact opposite of how I had been feeling for the last couple of weeks. I couldn't wait till I got home and got that box out of my truck!

Quantum mechanics proves that we can influence things on the atomic and molecular level, it proves it! Think of crystals, how atomically ordered their structures are. Now think if you held one in your hand saying, "I feel like crap, I feel like crap," over and over, what would you feel when you picked up that crystal? Doesn't that explain haunted houses? If you always went into the same room to cry, everyday for a year, wouldn't someone who went in there feel sad? Well, I had a box of Tom in my truck and it wasn't fun.

I had talked to my friends on the way home, (my phone working and not working), calling one after another. I found out I could clear the energy of crystals a few different ways. By burying them in the ground, by letting them sit overnight in sea salt water, and by leaving them in moonlight.

Don't ask me, I was learning and none of this, I had heard before. I stopped on the way home and got two packages of sea salt and filled up a five gallon bucket with water and dumped that salt in there. Anxiously, I put the crystals in the there as quick as I could, one after another, ugh, get them away from me. I wanted to kick the box over and run screaming into my house and never open the door again. Ha-ha that's the way it felt. While transferring the crystals, I came across two different items that I just hated from the moment I saw them. One was a little red bag made of some sort of cloth, and the other was a long black tubular type of crystal that just didn't look right. I threw them in the back of my truck and ran into the house to wash my hands once I was done. I knew I wasn't going to save those items.

That bucket sat in my driveway for a month before I took anything out of it.

I let the moonlight, sea salt, hocus pocus and whatever else clear those damn things, before I touched them again! That night I went to Angels Sanctuary and as a Shaman walked in, I held out that black crystal as he walked by and said, "Dude, check this out." His reply of, "Get that fucking thing away from me," told me I was right and I threw it in the bed of my truck again. After hearing, "Where is Tom tonight," for the 700th time, I told them what had happened. They all seemed a little sad at his demise in spirituality. He really was a charming guy. I would often think of him and wonder how he was doing and every once and awhile I would call him just to talk and tell him stuff.Even for a concrete worker, somehow, (I guess because I liked him) ,it hurt a little bit to have our friendship die. I could also see that it served its purpose of getting me to know the Shamans. Still, I felt bad, especially since it ended on the note of him considering me, "evil." When I told him about the bag that I didn't like, he said, "That's because it was made for me by a witch to repel demons, that's why you don't like it, because it feels the demon in you." My reply of, "Will you listen to what you just said to me. It was made by a witch to fight demons," elicited no response and a quick end to the conversation.

That black rock was a crappy little thing as well. I didn't want to touch itagain, I just left it in the bed of my truck and went about my business.

For a few weeks following this, while meditating, I kept thinking about making a staff. Every day I would think, "I should make a staff." Nothing amazing, just the simple thought would run through my head over and over again. So one day, following impulse, I took a ride down to Coggers and looked around and cut down a good tree. When I got back to my truck, it was dead, it wouldn't start. My very first thought was, "That fucking rock is still in the bed." I took it and the red bag to the top of the hill and buried them then and there. Later I found out my starter had died, on a brand new vehicle, my starter had died. The truck was three months old. All I could think was, "That damn rock." Surprisingly enough, once I got rid of that crystal, my electrical problems ceased after that. I'm not saying my phone never shut off again by itself, but infrequently. I think there's a certain type of spirit that interferes with electrical equipment, because it's happened to me a few times since and usually after I've dealt with a crappy space.

I took the small tree I had cut down home. Well, every night I would put my kids to bed and work on it. I first peeled the bark and then would meditate into it, holding it in my hands, one hand next to another. I started at the bottom, and would move up to a different place every night until after a month I had gone all the way to the top and I started my way back down. I meditated into every inch of that wood. After about two weeks of effort, the wood split. Dammit! That was a lot of work for nothing, but still, I just knew, I was meant to make a staff.

I laughed about it when I told it to the Shamans, I remember one of them asking me if I had gotten permission from the tree, (which sounded weird), I mean, how one sided is that conversation? "Excuse me, Mr. Tree, do you mind if I cut you down?"

"No Norman, I would be delighted to have you end my life, cut short, (pun intended), my existence, have at it chum, but please, use a good saw."

Ask permission? Riiiight. Buuuut, since I hadn't and my staff had split, I decided to give it a shot. I went back down to Cogs and walked around, until I found a likely looking candidate. I placed my hands on the trunk and asked for permission. Since I didn't feel anything, or hear anything, and the tree didn't start talking like one of the Ents from Lord of the Rings, I cut it down. Once I had, I found it was already dead and waiting for me. That staff has served me well since.

CHAPTER 11

So Tom was convinced I was evil. I continued talking with my friends and started taking "Shaman class" on Saturdays as well. This was a great time in my life because I was completely open to everyone and everything. I think you could have sold me London Bridge back then if you were a fast enough talker. That is, if you only wanted 10 bucks for it.

The changes that had been wrought in my life, by the healing, started showing everywhere else as well. With my kids, with my ex wife and my ex fiancé, even work stopped bothering me as much. One day on the job site, one of my co-workers said, "Sorry about stressing you out," because I had just watched him freak out about something. I mean "freak out", where he was screaming at the top of his voice at someone while the customer looked on. I had looked him in the eye and said, "You will never stress me out again."

I mean why? I looked back and saw how foolish I had been over the last 10 years. Getting worried, stressing out over decorative concrete, the people I worked with, over things I thought I wanted. Why? When I finally cashed my ticket in, all the pool decks I had poured wouldn't amount to a hill of beans. In the end, not one ounce of concrete would matter, and not one of my co-workers would be there guiding me to the light. I knew there was a spirit world and none of them spoke of, or projected worries about concrete. So honestly, why bother? But more importantly, hindsight showed me all I had worried about, all the stress and frustration and hard times in life, times where I felt alone and empty inside had also served to get me here.

    I cannot state that more or clearly enough. Once again, my command of the English language fails me. I realized, that all the problems I had had, were to bring me to a point where I felt I had to ask for help. Once there, help was just waiting for me, but I had to ask first! Most importantly, I had to mean it. I began to look back and see all the hardships I had suffered were for a purpose. I could clearly see the lessons these times where meant to teach, and by learning those, I could see the next lessons. Everything I had worried about had turned out ok. All I had stressed about had been for no reason!

    Imagine for a moment, if you could look at something from afar and watch its progress. You can see that the boulder it encounters hides a beautiful bend in the road. That ultimately it will reach its goal and the road it was on was clearly defined, but that seeing only what was in front of it, it couldn't perceive the ultimate destination. Well that was what I felt. All the worries and stress I had been through had been only something I had done to myself. Think about it. No one can stress you out; you choose to react that way. I can say anything I want to you, but ultimately you choose to be bothered, or not. The perfection of creation is that we exercise one of the greatest powers in the universe.

Choice.

Most of us, we choose poorly and selfishly. Worry? I saw that we never ever get anything from worry. All we do is make ourselves feel miserable and those around us as well. I knew that if I had put all those times I worried to better use, like meditating for instance, well I would be levitating here, over my chair as I type this. I guess the easiest way to say it would be, I started to see the perfection in life. The perfection in my life and seeing it my life, I could see it in all lives. I began to be thankful for it, I started to trust even more. I would say, "If I died tomorrow, I would die with a smile in my heart because I felt true love."

This is from a guy who took bronze in the complaining division at the 1984 winter Olympics. I had this grin that couldn't be erased from my face. The more I thought about my past, and remembered that moment in the Mansion, the wider my grin became. Once I began to detach from the drama of things, I began to see the motivations of the people behind them. Work? Ha. Never again would I let my boss wind me up. I could see that he was just stressed out, and he got off on making others feel a fraction of that stress. If you have a boss like that, understand, the only way they know how to feel better, it to make others feel like them.(Sad when you think about it.) I began to see how I used to choose to let him make my day frustrated. I started laughing at him when he was irate, because to me, he was getting worked up over losing money, and in the next life, what the hell was, "That job I did came out perfect," going to get me? It was all so unimportant to me. I remember one morning telling him, "Look at you, you're miserable, it's 5:30 a.m. and you're already miserable. How's the rest of your day going to be?" Ha ha. From riding me, he muttered to himself and walked away.

I saw that all of our lessons in life come from suffering. It's a sad and true fact of the human condition. We don't have the best day ever and say, "I'm never doing that again." No, we suffer, and learn or we don't.

Choice.

If we are knuckleheads, then we don't learn, and repeat again. How many of us have friends who say, "Why does this keep happening to me????" Well, because you can't see beyond what you want to, what you're supposed to learn. When you can start to see that what you've suffered was for your own personal growth, then you stop worrying about suffering and begin to trust. I knew, absolutely, that what I had been through had served purpose. Therefore, I knew that whatever I might go through again in the future would do the same. I started looking at life differently too. I had been through the fire, and while I came out a little crusty and singed, I was alive, and I had my kids. What more could I want? I told people, "If you are very, very lucky, you will have 36,500 days on the earth, that's it! I can count to that number in about three hours. At the end of those 36,000 days, you don't want to say, I had 20,000 bad days, hell, I don't even want to say, I had 1,000, bad days. Life is too short, too sweet and too good to have a bad day, since we choose it, have a good day." Personally, I've already had like 8,000 bad days, so I refuse to have anymore.

This was a huge change from that whiny guy that would blame others for his problems of before.

So no more Tom, but I had the Shamans that I talked to everyday. I was just so pumped. In such a good mood, driving around, talking and laughing. When people would ask me, "How are you?"my reply was always, "Kicking in the high vibe baby!" It felt like I had spent 10 years working at a project, and I was finally done. That was the level of satisfaction I had. And it seemed like every day I was learning something new, every single moment, there was something to notice. Whether it was paying attention to the animals that I saw and the messages they represented, or noticing the little signs that were everywhere. The more I was open to it, the more I saw. I realized that God is always trying to get our attention, we just never listen.

    One morning I stopped for coffee at the gas station like I usually did on my way to work, and as I was getting rung out, I said, "Have a nice day, nice man," to the clerk. His reply, "I'm not a nice guy, "made me feel bad for him. I walked out and thought to myself of what to say to him the next time I saw him. I really felt bad, how shitty does your life have to be to answer like that? As I drove down the road, I felt my heart chakra open. It was like, I sensed a click in my heart, and all of sudden my chest felt two feet wider. It was the strangest thing, and as I drove up 495 North, I was laughing saying, "My fucking heart is open" at 5:15 a.m. All those weeks with the Shamans, they had been telling me, "Open your heart." Then asking me, "Do you feel that?" and I, lying about it answering yes. Well, here it was 5:00 a.m. and I felt it!

    The next morning the clerk was outside having a smoke as I was leaving. I said to him as I walked past, and lit up a butt of my own, "You know, sometimes life is hard and we make mistakes, but that mean you are not a nice person."

"No, I'm not a nice person because I'm really into black magic and the dark arts," was his reply.

    "Cool man, I'm studying to be a Shaman, there's so much out there to learn." I answered, puffing contentedly.

"Nice, dude, do you know there's a cemetery in Worcester that you can go and talk with the devil?" He was looking at me intently.

Thinking of something a Shaman had said, I replied"Hmm, it says in the Bible that Jesus rebuked the devil, I think that means he wouldn't even acknowledge him." The big guy just walked away.

"Well, really there is no duality, so ultimately, nothing is evil." He said to me, bringing up a large argument I had, had with myself.

"Of course there is. That's wrong, there is duality, something either serves God or it doesn't, it cannot be clean, and dirty at the same time."

He started twitching, honest to God, his shoulders twitched and he didn't even seem to notice it.

"Well I am a soul collector and I have like 10,000 souls."

"Sweet, what a nice day it's going to be," I said as I took a drag on my butt.

"I was Jack the Ripper in a previous life and Hitler and Lancelot."(I don't know how Lancelot came in that mix).

I just looked at him and smiled and said, "I don't care whether or not you worship frogs, as long as you are happy."

By this time, he was tweaking out. Seriously, he was standing five feet away from me, and his shoulders were rocking in jerks, like someone was punching him. He was totally oblivious to it. Honestly, he did not realize he was moving. That was the strangest thing. He kept talking, but as I looked at him, I could see these dark shadows crossing his face. That's the only way I can describe it, these dark highlights that kept moving around. I thought to myself,"Holy shit, he's got like three things attached to him, and they ain't happy lovey." He kept telling me how powerful he was, and I kept nodding in agreement saying,"That's cool man," and watching him bipping and bapping without realizing it. It was very strange. Eventually I had to go to work and as I drove up 495 at 80mph, I kept thinking about how calm I felt, and how freaked out he was. I thought of the darkness that feeds from your desires, wants and fears. How it makes you feel, how it feeds from you, and how like all darkness, it doesn't like the light. I felt so calm, so collected; Ricky was doing the herky jerky. There's the difference.

    Over time,the weird, darkart practicing gas station clerk has become a friend of mine. I still see him every morning. He's a good, confused guy, and from what I can see he has a kind heart and really is a nice man. I realized that whatever was hanging around him, got off on making people afraid. He enjoyed shocking people, and since I was just sitting there, feeling good, and feeling love, not afraid, it couldn't stand it.

    When I talked about it later with my new friends, I was told he had spirits "attached" and upon further questioning, I learned that some spirits canattach themselves to us. To feed from our energy, to hang around, to amuse themselves, really, who knows? I was told that they could be physically felt by a pain on the left side of the neck. As someone who had dealt with the spirit world his whole life, and suffered from chronic neck pain, that rang true for me. That's what the purpose of smudging was, to help break that attachment. I used to think my neck pain was from stress, or from driving and holding my phone with my shoulder all the time.As I talked to the Shamans about it and rubbed my neck, I realized that I hadn't felt that pinching neck pain in weeks. Eventually I came to learn that it was a great warning sign. If I was in a bad mood, and I checked, chances are, my neck was tight, (yeah, yeah Norman, of course, you're stressed, naturally your muscles will tighten and your neck WOULD hurt if you were in a bad mood). Yet when my neck hurt, I would call my friends up, joke, laugh, be goofy, and generally have fun and it quickly went away. I can't tell you the number of times in the future where I would pull something off of someone and feel it run up my arms and all of sudden get a massive neck pinch. I get ahead of myself.

Since I knew the spirits were made of energy, I decided I needed to learn what I could about energy itself. I had heard numerous people talk about Reiki, which I learned was a form of energy work. Well, what better way to learn about energy than to learn about a type of energy healing? I asked Susan who was a teacher and she agreed to give me the level 1 and 2 attunements. My understanding was, that to become a Reiki practitioner, you received attunements. There were/are 3 steps, level 1 and 2 and the master level in which you can then give others the attunements and make them Reiki practitioners. We set it up for the following week at her place. The night before I was to learn, I went out on a date and ended up splitting three bottles of wine with my companion. As I drove up to Portsmouth the following day, my head was pounding with a hangover and I thought about cancelling, just driving home and climbing into my bed for the day. Just as everything that has been important in my life, there was a moment of choice, where crappy Norman said, "Nah, I don't wanna."

I am glad I didn't. Since the Susan was pretty, even if I was bored I could stare at her and pretend to be interested in Reiki. I really didn't know what to expect, but I knew I was lucky because I was getting a one on one class with her. It didn't take long to see, and more importantly to feel, that this was something I was supposed to be doing.

Again, I was open to new things, so no one was going to shock me or make me say, "Are you kidding me?" At Angels Sanctuary I had conversations after conversations about aliens, bigfoot, everything under the sun. I had someone look at me and say, "You know when we die, we are going to be born on EARTH 2 to give this earth a chance to rest." I had developed this innate ability to keep a perfectly straight face while the voice in the back of my head was saying, "Wtf???" A simple class about energy was a breeze. So I was attentive, open with her and I enjoyed it thoroughly. Susan was and is very easy to get along with, spontaneous and outspoken. She made me laugh often, since she surprised me a lot with random observations that just popped out. After being taught a bunch of things about the history of Reiki and how to use it, I received the attunement. The Reiki attunement process was different from anything I had experienced. I am not going to go into it here, since hundreds of books have been written about Reiki, but when she was done, my headache was gone and the palms of my hands were tingling like no tomorrow.

I was a Reiki practitioner, yay! And I started using it everywhere and on everyone I could. My poor children were my best test subjects. When they had a headache or felt pain, Dad would lay his hands on them and close his eyes and feel the energy flowing. Sometimes it aggravated them, sometimes it didn't. I remember when my son fell off the top of a slide onto his tailbone onto concrete. After a three hour emergency room visit, upon arriving home, I told him, turn over I will do Reiki on you.

"No way dad!"

I guess he was thinking I was going to put my hands on his rear. After settling him on his back, I explained how I didn't have to touch the area but that the Reiki would flow to wherever it was needed most. He let me, and very quickly his pain went away. Soon, other people with ailments started asking me to help them. I'm not going to go into every detail, but two things regarding Reiki stand out. One, my niece who had suffered from a chronic wrist injury and saw a specialist in Boston for it on a regular basis needed help. A week after doing Reiki on her, she went back to him with no pain and while he didn't understand it, he told her to come back in a year for a follow up visit. Secondly, one day while driving, the school nurse called and said hesitantly,"Your son is here with a headache, he says you're a Reiki master, do you want to talk to him?" Ha-ha how great is that?

Given the Reiki and all the other people I was able to help in my own way, I started to love life again. It was so much better than the,"Get the fuck out of my way," existence I had been living the last ten years. I began to realize if I spent my whole life pouring concrete, if I made something like the pyramids, how could that compare to helping someone? What greater good could I serve in my life? What is the potential butterfly effect of helping someone? I knew that if I did something that changed someone's life, then maybe they could do the same to someone else, spreading good, etc., etc. I couldn't hope for anything better than that. As I talked to the Shamans they told me it was called, "a life in service to others." It's not by pouring concrete, but by offering kind words, or making them laugh. Being able to run energy and move some pain from their body. Nothing to me is more rewarding, nothing felt better than to give. The more I thought about my transformation, the wider and wider that grin on my face would get, and more and more I felt happy inside.

One night the Shamans had a Christmas party. I was standing out by a fire in the yard. As I contemplated the flames, a couple joined me. I started talking about how good life was and how everything was perfect. Since I was sincere, they could feel it, and as I talked, they got closer and looked at each other and ended up holding hands and smiling along with me. They told me they were going through a divorce and as I talked, instead of being bitter to each other, they saw that they had served purpose t and that their time together was done. If only for five minutes, I helped them, if only for a moment I made them look past resentment, to look towards each other in a loving manner again. How rewarding do you think that felt? As a divorcee, I could appreciate it.

Eventually I started studying with the "Head Shaman" himself. Where before most of the people I had been speaking with were his students. My questions and insights led me to things only he could answer. After a few short conversations, I decided he was an excellent person. He showed me that spirituality wasn't being perfect. You could be a man and still be spiritual, and even the most spiritual people I knew still had things to overcome. Perfection was limited to heaven; we on earth have to struggle with our faults. Once I was at his house with a couple of others. I had just met this great woman named Laura, and I was making her smile and laugh. All of a sudden her phone rang and as I watched her talking, I could see her face change and drop as she got upset and aggravated. It was a horrible transformation to behold, like watching a rose die. I felt so bad that as I looked at her, I could only wish her love and happiness. All of sudden the Shaman, who was facing the other direction turned to me and asked, "Did you just open your heart?"

"Yeah."

"Huh." And he went back to talking. I was amazed he felt what I did.

I realized I had a lot to learn from him and that made me open to everything he had to teach. The head Shaman became my friend and my teacher and I spoke with him every day. He was and is very powerful man energy wise, and from faking stuff when he said, "Do you feel that?" I started to really feel the energy when he worked on me or gave me attunements. Since it was winter and I got laid off from work (can't pour concrete in the winter, thank the Lord), I had a lot more time to meditate and to study. And every day I would bring my kids to school and go to the gym and come home and meditate.

The more I learned about energy, the more I understand about the spirit world. As someone who was practicing Reiki every day, and doing energy based meditation, the spirit world was going cuckoo at my place. Naturally the house where I lived was very haunted and I used to hear insane amounts of tapping. More importantly, I learned that I could feel energy. As I sat on my couch and meditated, I would often hear a tap from the kitchen and physically feel it, (I cannot describe it simpler than that), this led me to start questioning why, etc., etc. When I was in a customer's house and I heard the same kind of tap and felt it as well I would ask myself, "Did I bring that spirit with me? Or was it here and it's letting me know it's here?" Since I was smudging every day, I like to think it was the latter.

CHAPTER 12

So I began to learn, and every day I would speak to my friends, the Shamans. A member of their circle had dropped out so there was a place for me. It was great because as I started developing my own gifts and things unfolded, I could call and talk about it to them and get opinions. I began to help people as well. I had always been that sympathetic ear for friends and now I began to take that to the next step and people would seek me out to talk to me. What a difference from previously, where no one wanted to be around me. The changes wrought by the healing really began to show in every aspect of my life. My relationship with my kids had never been better and all the things they would do didn't bother me as much, (you know kids). I felt calmer, and while I was and am Dad, I didn't get angry as easily.

My work was starting to turn and I really began to bring sales in. People like when their salesman smiles, laughs and gives off that peaceful, confident energy. I was so calm, nothing anyone could say would take me out of that place. Let me tell you they tried, trust me, but everything I had once thought important, I realized was nothing. It seemed like everything I experienced now in my life had meaning and purpose, and because I was looking, I started seeing it all. I kept hearing the Shamans say I was, "coded," which meant that I had innate abilities and they were only waiting there to be activated. The head Shaman used to say, "Think that you lived a thousand lives, and you placed things along your path to help you remember; you're finding those things!" And while they might seem a little crazy to you, they resonated with me, because that was exactly what it seemed like was occurring.

One night I was online and Googling, "Chakra meditation." I learned that what I had taught myself was a legitimate meditation and an extremely powerful one. How perfect? It was a million things like that, things began to steer this Titanic to safer waters. Individually, these were small, but taken as an aggregate, huge.

Then one day, it happened. I woke up and I could fly, I could levitate around the room and hover in places for more than three hours. Then I found I could levitate objects with the power of my mind.

Sorry, not yet, just making sure you're paying attention.

I continued going to "Shaman classes" with everyone else and learned so much. Guided meditation really is amazing in what it can show you about yourself. Sitting there, listening to the beating drum, following the leader's voice, I saw many insights. Oftentimes it wouldn't be things I would want to share with the class afterwards, sometimes it was. I looked forward to those four-hour classes once a month. But Monday nights at Angels Sanctuary were my favorite, sitting in the "healing circle" in our backjacks. I usually made everyone laugh and got away with being my obnoxiously goofy self. It was like one big happy screwed up loving family. A line of hugs would await me when I got there, a line of people wanting to talk and share and care about each other.

Usually people are pulled on a spiritual path for a reason. Out of a hundred people to suffer divorce, bankruptcy, extra child support and everything else I had been through. Most of them would turn to alcohol, drugs and be asking their "personal health care provider" for something to ease their mind. Maybe five of them would be lucky enough to see purpose in what had happened. Maybe two of those five would begin to use their experiences positively to help others. I was one of those two and I felt special. Now at Angels Sanctuary, here were 30 people, who like me had been through the fire. They all had problems in life, but they were all openhearted and sympathetic to one another. It was amazing to go there and be hugged by 15 people who felt love for me, who valued my opinion. What a difference from my past and what I was accustomed to at my job. Seriously, if you ever have a bad day, just have 10 people hug you, one after the other. Your day will be much better afterwards, take my word for it. I began looked forward to those Monday nights with my group of likeminded souls. It seemed that every direction I turned in, I was helping people. At the store in line, letting co-workers vent, " I don't know why I am telling you this, but, " became a common phrase. I remember one day talking to some people I had just met and explaining how everything in our lives served purpose. They were stressed out and worried. As I stood there, with that goofy grin pasted on my face, I could see that I was touching them. Here I was helping them see it was ok, that worrying got you nothing, and that it ultimately, whatever they were concerned about, served to teach them. I remember the man saying to me, "It's been said that nothing can wipe the grin off the face of an enlightened man." And that is how I felt. Enlightened and at peace with myself.

 What an amazing difference, from previous years where, "Get out of my way," was my motto. Now, if I was going to be late to a sales appointment, I started trusting that it was perfect. That maybe my lateness would save my life from an accident, or someone else's. I could see the perfection in my life and I trusted in it implicitly.

 Talking to the head Shaman I found he was the same way. That was one of the things that struck me about him, we had a lot in common. He would tell me how scared he was as a kid or a young adult, and I could sympathize, because I knew what it was like. No one else would understand that, no one else who hadn't heard something tap on the bedroom door, listen to it walk around the bed and feel the bed sag as the spirit sat down next to me, would understand that fear. Well, he did and I was grateful for it. Every morning I could call him, talk about what I had seen and learned the day before and get his opinions.

My work really paid off because I made my own schedule and drove 50,000 miles a year. I had a lot of time to process what I had noticed, and a lot of time to call and talk to my friends. Let me say this outright. I always had my own opinions. I would call them, and talk about something I had experienced, but ultimately, I would have my own beliefs, even if I kept them to myself. The head Shaman could tell me that every time I felt a chill run down my back that it was my spirit guides touching my energy to confirm what I thought. Personally, I noticed that it always happened after I thought something. Like I said mentally, "spirits attach themselves to people," and then I would get a chill. I thought it was my energy field resetting itself to show my new belief, others thought it was something else. Again, I have this amazing gift where I can nod and keep a stupid look of belief on my face while people tell me the strangest of things, and it came in handy during that period. One of the things I didn't agree with the Shamans was, the whole non-duality thing.

You see, a lot of people, especially the ones I knew, believe there is no evil, things just are. There is no good and bad, only things that serve God. I was told, "even evil acts from a place of love," meaning that it believes in what it does is right. I don't agree. Evil is stupid, and it exists. So when people would say this to me, I would nod and smile and look stupid, and think, "no fucking way." I've seen evil, and bad things, I knew they existed. Now I do believe that God uses peoples choices to further his plans, but non-duality implies that evil is God's work, that smells to me.

The group started inviting me to meetings they were having and to investigations they were going on. The meetings were the head Shaman sitting there in the dark, channeling a higher vibration spirit. The members would sit around and listen to it, and start asking questions. Again, we go back to that gift that I have where I can keep a perfectly straight face.

Here's what I think about channeling. The spirit world always has its own agenda. Some are nice and some aren't. The person who is channeling basically opens him or herself up, and lets a spirit speak through them. If you don't believe in ghosts, then this is an even further push for you, but bear with me for the sake of the story. The channeler is kind of a door for the spirit world to talk to us. Now, I've had people tell me, "I channeled Jesus," or "this is Moses speaking," (straight face thing again), and then gone on to pass messages to me or others with me. I've never ever had a person who is channeling say,"Tomorrow at noon, a leaf will fall on your head, or a robin will poop on your shoulder," and had it happen. Usually it's, "You need to keep an open mind about blah blah," or some other generic spiritual advice. Again, I say, the spirit world has its own agenda, and as someone who felt the touch of God in his heart and was healed of years of shittiness in three seconds, I can honestly say, we suck.

Something divine has such pure intention, such pure energy, that in the face of it, we are horrible. All those wants, selfish thoughts, greedy things we think of, the divine possesses none of them. Because its purity, you would be made aware of your own impurities and you couldn't handle it. It's like me standing next to Brad Pitt. Hey, I'm a good looking guy, but I would be thinking, "Shit, I need to work out more," or "I need $4 million in plastic surgery to look as good as him." I don't think that you could speak with the divine. It would drop you to your knees, in recognition of your flaws. I know, 3 seconds of divine love in a haunted mansion wiped out 10 years of cynicism. So for someone to say, "I am channeling Jesus," it really made and makes me wonder. What is pretending to be Jesus, and what kind of message does it really have for us?

So even though I had all my own opinions, I kept them to myself. Pretty soon I started getting invited to investigations with the Shamans. It was fun to go to someone's house, listen to them talk about spirits and then walk around, feel and sense. Afterwards, we would all talk about what we had felt and picked up on, we would hold hands and combine energies. The head Shaman would lead us in prayer, utilizing what we had all sensed. If I had walked in a room and detected anger and frustration, I would tell the others and then they would try to follow that to see if they felt anything. Eventually what would come out, was a prayer designed specifically for whatever we encountered. Its sole purpose was to try to cross the spirits. That's what I was told I was doing, crossing spirits. I was informed that spirits or ghosts that were here, were stuck in this realm. It might be for any one of a variety of reasons, but that they were here on the earth realm and not going to heaven. So to cross a spirit, you either make it understand that the reasons it remained here were invalid, or you held love in your heart and transmuted its emotions

I know how it sounds, but basically, that's what it is.

One of my talents is that I would ask very direct questions, ones that made the Shamans uncomfortable occasionally. When someone told me she is guided to do something, I asked, "Do you hear the voice? Or is it in your head?" It was in her head, which is ok and good, but different from actually hearing a voice. When the head Shaman told me that he sees a door for the spirits to go into, I asked, "Do you actually see the door? Or is it in your head?" He told me he saw the door and that it was wonderful.

Personally, I don't think you can cross a spirit. I mean, how arrogant is that? To me, it really is a spiritual ego trap. A spirit has been here for 50 years, or 300, feeling angry and you're going to come in and get them to go to heaven? In two hours? In one hour? In 15 minutes of feeling love and light? A few times we did investigations and the people would call up and claim to still be hearing things. We would go back and the Shamans would say, "You brought more home with you, it's you, attracting spirits, they are attaching to you and following you home." While there is a degree of truth in this, I don't think that's why people were still hearing things. I think we just weren't doing what we thought we were doing. To me, crossing a spirit is just a perfectly human thing to do. Try and help where we know nothing about. Who says the spirit world even needs help? Has anyone ever thought of that?

Now I know with an open heart we can accomplish almost anything. I think that a lot of the time what we were physically feeling in the prayer circle, was the spirit walking into our energy fields and attaching there. Inevitably, the next day after an investigation we would talk and the head Shaman would always ask, "Who took home the _____" because it wasn't that we were crossing the spirits, it was that we were allowing them into our energy fields. That's how we were supposedly clearing houses. Allowing them to attach to us, and once there, you had to be damn sure to stay in a good mood, since they were basically energy leeches. All a spirit does is project, well, whatever its dysfunction is, it's going to project it at you. Since I had learned that an open heart was kryptonite to the crappy things, the only way to get rid of them was to stay happy, stay in the high vibe. Think of it, if I am a spirit trying to feed of off anger, and I attach to someone because they are bright with energy. Well, unless I get that anger, eventually I get sick of it and drop off. I cannot explain it better than that. Some spirits feed from dysfunctions, some want you to be afraid, and some want you to be angry, because all of these emotions are energies for them to feed from. Others are benign and loving and want good for you, (more about them later). Whatever the deal is, there is always a purpose behind it.

  The head Shaman had a great story he always told at houses we went to investigate. "I used to play in a band, at bars and I would see spirits hanging around people telling them to have another beer. If I am an alcoholic and love beer, well, when I die, I can't drink anymore. Since beer and the act of drinking is an energy, the next best thing to drinking, is hanging around someone who does, and tell them all the time, "drink a beer drink a beer," over and over. Eventually they drink to the point that they black out and then the spirit takes over their body. That's why people do crazy nasty things during blackouts." I agreed with that because I had seen people in the middle of possession, and had seen how the spirit tried to snap their mind. Think of it, if you feel something trying to take you over, you don't know what it is, or what's going on, just that you feel cold, and are afraid. It gets in deeper and makes you more afraid until your mind just snaps. Then who's driving? I know that some spirits are like parasites, feeding from negativity, feeding from the weak, and the whole time, the people are unaware of it. To them, it's just coming across as a thought process, to them it's just that little voice in their head that says, "Smoke some weed," or, "steal that," All the spirit cares about is energy that you create or get by doing so, or some enjoy just making someone else as crappy as them, it wants company. Ever notice how people love when someone else does something bad as they do? Well it's a lot like that.

Is it any wonder how the innocuous turns evil or addiction gets worse and worse? The more you do something, the more energy it gets from it and the more it's able to influence you. My house when I was married was extremely haunted. At first, the spirit was only able to turn off the TV but after making me afraid for months every night. It had enough energy to move objects around. Again, it is my belief that most spirits feed from energy. While I do believe this, I also know that the perfection of creation is choice. You can have a whole room full of friends telling you to smoke weed, ultimately it is you who smokes it, not them. So I am not explaining away anyone's poor behavior, merely trying to bring to light what can affect it.

So we would go to a house and talk to the homeowners about the spirit world and try to make them less afraid. Many, many people are and were afraid of ghosts, but usually after speaking with them about our beliefs, and seeing how calm we were, they tended to be less so. We would walk from room to room, sense and feel and find out which place felt heaviest. Then we would gather there with the homeowners and say a prayer and take home the spirits. I might have done this about ten times with the group. Sometimes I felt beat up that night, or the following day. I would have to work hard to get myself in that good loving space, to drive away what was around me, sometimes I didn't. I continued to go to class and see things while in guided meditation learning about myself. Once, while I was in meditation, I started feeling an electrical charge on my hand. That's exactly what it felt like, electricity running from my pinky finger to the middle of my hand, maybe an inch long, over and over. At first I thought it was a minute muscle spasm, but nothing moved on my hand. As I stood outside during our break, chuffing down a smoke, the head Shaman came out and I explained what was happening. "Well of course, you moron, you're a healer." I smiled and thought to myself, "This is so cool."

Life was good. I got Susan to go to a couple of Shamans classes with me. She came mostly I think because she could see the progress I was making. She did and once, while she was sitting next to me during meditation, I saw her grab at her hair and fling something off onto the floor. I looked at her and then at the floor. Then I honestly felt something crawling up my legs. When I asked her what she did, she told me she had felt something crawling around on her crown for a few weeks and she flung it off. When I told her what I had felt, she laughed, patted my cheek and quickly changed the subject.

I also began to have a social life again. I remember I had met this woman online and we went out to dinner. We went back to her house and because I was so in the zone and open, I could see through the meaning of everything she was saying to me, every question. I could see the purpose behind her comments, (something normally completely hidden from us men), and as I looked at her and smiled and answered her question perfectly, I felt her heart open.

It was to me, the coolest thing, because I actually felt something from someone else, not sensing, but something tangible. You will hear that a lot along the path of spirituality, an open heart, or open your heart or if you are with me, "Open your haahtya knucklehead." Let me give you a great example of what I am talking about. When I used to pray, I would always ask God to take my life and spare my children's if it was ever needed, (hey man, I love my kids unconditionally, of course I would die for them). Well, when I would ask this, I would feel like my heart was about to come out of my chest and part of me would think, "Oh crap, tonight? You want it now?" Well, that was my heart opening. To me and others, it feels like your heart is going to burst from your chest. When I was in the mansion and God touched my heart, he opened it, and because he is the man, it made it easier for me to open it afterwards.

Laying on this lady's couch, giving her the perfect answer, I felt her heart open. It was like all of a sudden, my heart doubled in size, just like that. A lot of the techniques the Shamans taught me was getting the heart open and using it as a tool to heal, to open others. For example, if your arm hurts, well I place my hand there and feel the energy of it, (Remember, I don't sell granola, this is a real thing), and then feel my heart and match the feeling there, or I pull it into my heart and change it. It works, the spirit world confirms it. **PLAY HEALER EVP** So I feel her heart open, and I say, "Holy shit I just felt your heart open." Naturally, she looks at me like I have three heads, but I didn't care, I had felt her heart. The following week, I had a date with Susan on Monday and I was supposed to see this same woman on Tuesday. Susan comes over and doesn't leave. When I took her out for dinner the next day, I asked, "You know I had a date tonight don't you?"

"I am a professional psychic, what do you think? Why do you think I am still here?"

Ha ha, what a great woman and honestly, what a great thing to say. In that statement she let me know she could and would know if I was up to anything and from that moment on, I was crazy about her. She and I started dating. She was a lot of fun and still had a natural innocence about her. Even just going over her house to hang out, I learned so much from her. We dated for quite a while. She is an extremely powerful woman, the master of many healing modalities. I never understood why she was afraid of the spirit world the way she was. The thing is, because she was so gifted and knew so much, she was bright to ghosts, and therefore always attracting things to herself. She would put up protections to shield her. By doing so, this invited something in to break them and learn something new, and so on and so forth. She was always pulling things from people, always attracting spirits.

Always, that's what happens, the more spiritual you are, the more you attract, and since she was afraid, she was always attracting crappy things that fed from fear, to her. We talked for hours about it and sometimes she would get it, and then she wouldn't. It was like hot and cold. Sometimes she would listen and not be afraid, then something creepy would happen that would test her faith and she would be scared for her life. She would always get crystals and say,"Look at this, this helps keep the spirits away," and because of her belief, it would for a bit. Then her belief would waver, and she would feel evil about her again. I think she thought almost every spirit was evil. She couldn't see a flitting shape and not be fearful. I hope that one day she understands what it is about.

After that time at the Shamans class, where she flung that thing on the floor and I felt it crawl up my leg, it took me five months to get rid of that spirit. Every day I would feel it moving around on my head. Seriously, can you picture that? Whenever you have a moment to sit and be still, you feel something moving about on top of your skull. Do you have any idea what that is like? I alternately wish you did and you didn't. Even the Shamans weren't any help. Their advice didn't work at all. I would sit in meditation and feel it moving about, blocking me in my visualization. It was very frustrating. I tried every "white light" technique; sea salt baths, anything anyone would tell me. Eventually I figured out what to do, but it took a long time to get rid of it, and when I did, I was pretty thankful.

So here I was, open, healed, powerful and dating a pretty spiritual lady. I started back at work in the Spring and I was cranking in sales. Cranking! No longer was I frustrated by the busy, busy life. When I was running late, I trusted in the perfection of it. Simple as that. I started trusting that it was meant to be. Maybe my lateness would save a life, or serve another purpose. All I knew was that I didn't pound my fist on the dashboard at other drivers anymore.

I also started noticing signs. To me, looking for a sign, is like looking for God's messages to you, they are everywhere, but you need to have an open mind and look. Trust me, God wants to speak to you; he wants to let you know that he's there and around. Open your mind and your eyes, and look for them. Pick a manner, coins, numbers, animals, once you choose, begin to notice patterns and repetitions. From there, it's up to you to decipher them. Before the healing, I would look at other vehicles as I drove to a job site and notice pretty women. If I would see enough, I would think, "Oh I am going to have a good day today." Or, conversely, too few and I would assume I was in for a hard time. Now I know that the ease of my day depends on nothing but my own attitude, but that's a poor example of looking for signs.

For me, it became pretty apparent that birds and animals were the way I got messages. When I am feeling aggravated about something, I might see a deer that reminds me to be gentle with my approach to things. When I am feeling frustrated, I might see a finch which reminds me there's opportunities in everything. That's what I see, all the time. Because I look for them, I see them more and more. A couple of years ago, I was driving all day on the highway. Now, I was looking but I didn't see a single hawk. It was a frigid March day, so maybe they were smart and hiding or I just wasn't meant to see one. As I got on the highway, I saw someone hitchhiking. As I drove past, I could see that they were freezing and actually had a look of pain on their face. So I argued with myself for a bit, and then decided to get off the highway and turn around and help them out. As I got off the highway, there was a red tail hawk, flying above the off ramp. To me, that's a sign. If I hadn't decided to help that person out, I wouldn't have seen it. It's just that we get so wrapped up in life that we don't listen to God's messages. So caught up in our lives we forget that gift we all had as children, that the world loves us and wants our love back.

Another example:

I was in Billerica, MA for work at this customer's house. Since I was their salesman, I had gotten pretty close to them. They were a delightful couple, on the top end of middle age. Well, the husband had opened up to me and admitted to me his wife was really stressed about work. So I was on their stoop as she was coming home, and I started chatting with her. She was complaining about her work, about the people that she worked with, (hell I knew what that is like), and I started telling her perfect life was and how everything serves to teach us. As we were talking, I noticed something fall from a tree in the middle of the yard a few hundred feet away. It looked like a leaf or something, because it was slowly spinning its way towards us. So we were chatting and I was trying to help her and get her to see my point about life and out of the corner of my eye, I was watching this thing whirling towards us. Just as she was getting aggravated telling me how everyone there looked down on her, I interrupted her and reached out and this object landed right in my palm. I didn't even have to reach out that far merely, I put my hand out and it landed there. She looked at it with amazement and I saw it was a Blue Jay's feather. I said to her, "Do you know what Blue Jays stand for? Being in control of your emotions, and not letting them hurt others around you." I proceeded to tell her about how that related to her current situation, and I told her about how everything in our lives serves purpose, and not to stress out. To me, it was the greatest of satisfactions to know I was able make a slight difference in her day, just with that simple feather and God's help. That's what I mean about a sign.

I remember telling that to a friend and they got very irate and said, "I look at the bible for my messages, Jesus speaks to me and tells me what to do!"

"Then that's your way, not any better than mine, just different." I replied. Needless to say, the conversation went downhill.

Well, all of sudden as I started opening myself to it, I started seeing birds and feathers everywhere, and I started collecting them. Yay, whoopee, well, don't think I am walking around with bags of feathers or snaring innocent little birdies and plucking them. No, these found me. I would hear a voice say, take a walk, and there was a feather. Or "look down" and I would find something. Once, standing on the bank of the Hudson river in New York on a sunny summer's day. I was listening to hawks scream and feeling the wind on my face. My heart opened and I said to myself. "Thank you God, for this great gift of life," When I opened my eyes and looked down, I saw a turkey feather at my feet, literally at my feet. I had to laugh and then said, "You're just showing off now."

How cool is life?

CHAPTER 13

I first met Chris Wood during a ghost hunt tour of some factories in Leominster, MA with the Shamans. The group had been there the day before, walking the factories with the owner, who was a client of one of them. The ghost hunt was to be a huge fundraiser for the Shamans, so I invited a bunch of friends who I thought would be interested. Chris and his wife were invited by the head Shaman.

My role was to lead a group of people around this factory and teach them about the spirit world. It was an attempt by the Shamans to make the average person aware of ghosts and make some money doing so. Chris and his wife were part of that group that I led, whether by the head Shamans design or chance. From what I knew, the head Shaman had done some heavy duty spiritual work on him a few weeks prior and had told me that he saw me teaching him. So when he was part of the group I was supposed to lead, I wasn't surprised. Walking around and teaching people to feel and sense spirits around the factory was pretty fun and there are a lot of ghosts in there.

    Again, I am not going to go into someone else's story other than to say that I met Chris Wood there. He was slightly built, with a mop of almost Beatles hair. He had a great English accent and seemed extraordinarily pleased to meet me. I guess he had been told the same about me. I remember him saying, "I feel like I've known you for so long," after we had been chatting for about five minutes. Anyway, that night was fun and I got Chris' number and we agreed to meet the following week at some point. We met at his house with his wife, Sarah, also on hand. Though we had talked a little on the factory tour, it was there that I started to get to know Chris better. It was one of those great nights where conversation goes everywhere and we did a lot of spiritual things. I brought my drum and led him and his wife on a journey, (my first). More importantly, I enjoyed my time with them and I found Chris slightly fascinating. I'm not going to say he was a riddle wrapped in an enigma, but he was a complex guy, with an interest in the spirit world. Half Peruvian, half English, he was naturally spiritually inclined and had some experiences. After talking about it for a bit, we agreed to meet again soon and I was to start teaching him.

    That first journey was the start of a friendship that I continue to treasure to this day. He was and is a big hearted fellow with a lot of natural gifts. Whether it was from his foreign birth, or something else, he saw things differently than I did. I appreciated that quality a lot, because I was starting to get sick of the, "yes, yes," people that I kept encountering with the Shamans. Sometimes he aggravates me, sometimes he drives me a little cuckoo, but that is perfect because it teaches me more about myself. As agreed, a couple of weeks later, we got together so I could start teaching him. I am unique in a lot of ways, (hell I know I am), but with the spirit world, well, few have had more screwy experiences than I. Given the peace I felt about it and the absolute lack of fear, well, it was time to start paying back and teaching others. We met in Chelmsford and drove up the street to the cemetery where the Shamans and I had seen things some months previously. While we didn't see any spirits that night, he sensed a lot. That's so important, because feeling and being able to feel things is a large part of ghost hunting/spirituality. I remember us, sitting next to a tree, as I taught him to ground out energy. I kept having to tell him to ignore the mosquitoes that were buzzing us, (they kind of tended to leave me alone), because the more you fight something the worse it gets. Suddenly we both felt a cold spot come up on us. I told him to open up and see what he felt. His voice got excited as he described to me the different emotions he was sensing. Let me just say this, if I am sitting there in a good mood laughing and chatting with my friends, and all of a sudden I start feeling afraid, what's causing it? Did I suddenly decide to become afraid? Did my hypothalamus decide to inject nuclear peptides into my cellular structure and make me afraid? Now run the gamut of emotion and ask the same thing. Spirits project their drama at us. If you have been reading this, then you've already seen me say this 10 times, but it's as simple as that. If I am a spirit stuck on the other side working off anger issues, well, I will project that wherever I am at, (or feed from it), and that's why a lot of haunted houses give off an eerie feeling. You can be sure there is something in there, feeding on peoples' fear and getting a kick off of it, (and an energy charge). That was what we did with the Shamans. On the drive to wherever we were investigating, we would be laughing and joking and having fun. If you go somewhere haunted, all miserable and crappy, you're not going to sense any difference and chances are, you will come out feeling worse for the experience.

So he and I are under this tree on a perfect June night, talking and chatting, lazily swatting mosquitoes. I am sure he could see my grin even in the dark. All of a sudden we feel a cold spot and I tell him to tap into it, which is not more than letting your mind open up to something and paying attention to what you feel. So as he does this, he starts sensing all sorts of things from the spirit, and gets excited. I calm him down and tell him to go to his heart and feel love. I know it sounds so corny like that, but it's through our hearts that we change, (trust me on this), and can change energy. So it takes him a while but he does, and as soon as he does he says, "Nohm, I felt a rush of energy go up to my head."

Yes, he's English and calls me, "Nohm."

I tell him he has just crossed a spirit. "Fuuuuck," he says, "that's amazing." I then go through the process of describing how it is through our crown chakras that we connect with God and through that crown, when we transmute the energy, the spirit can go to God.

Congratulations Chris, you just crossed your first spirit.

Needless to say, he was pretty excited. After leaving there, I asked him if he wanted to feel one more thing, and we took a drive up the Training School. I don't know what made me think of that place; well I do, but at the time it surprised me. As we drove up, he yelled out loud and said, "I just felt someone run up to your truck screaming, that was horrible." He then grabbed the back of his neck and started rubbing. Ha-ha, I knew that trick and I told him that something had just attached to his energy field. "Don't worry, I will clear you before you go home." As we drove around, we stopped in front of the main building. Even in the dark and in the relative safety of the truck, it felt nasty. He told me,"All I hear is screaming,"and I agreed, the training school always felt crappy. Let me say this out right. This wasn't, "Ohh I think I sense something!" No this was, " HOLY SHIT, DID I MENTALLY SEE SOMEONE RUNNING AT THE TRUCK SCREAMING??" The kind of sensing that changes your view of the world. Being able to bring someone to that space was great, better still, to bring them out safe.

We finished our drive through, I talked about energy, how it feels, the changes and shifts in it. We spoke about what he had sensed, and the things he had felt, especially here, in the Training School. Eventually I brought him back to my house where we smudged and I cleared him.

Afterwards we had sex.

Of course we didn't. I'm just screwing with you and making sure you're reading this and not glancing through. I'm not gay. Never will be. Anyway, I was pretty excited because I took someone who, while fairly gifted, had experienced very little about the spirit world and helped him sense them.

So that the next day, when I called to check up on him, he was thanking me for my time and asking when we could do it again. I remember talking to the head Shaman about it. I was so excited because it seemed my first night teaching had gone perfectly, he was so happy for me. I remember walking though Shop and Save talking to him on my cell phone and him saying, "That's awesome man, love ya bro," and I felt it too and replied in kind. It was just the simple greater love that we all can have for each other, the simple love that we all "should" have for each other. Anyway, that was the last time I was ever that close, to that man.

Chris and I ended up meeting almost weekly after that. He had a great thirst for knowledge and I liked the sound of my own voice, so we were a perfect match. I kept wondering where to take him, I mean, it's not like haunted houses grow on trees. Cemeteries are cool and all, but I knew no one wants to think of people walking around in them at night. Really, think about it, besides ghost hunters, who would walk around in a cemetery at night? Then I realized, I had the perfect place, one that I knew was haunted as shit and one I had been trying to get the Shamans to go to for awhile now.

Coggers.

Hey want to learn of the spirit world? Let me take you to the most haunted place in North America to teach you! Coggers was perfect. The more I thought about it, the more sense it made and while I still had some trepidations about going down there to teach and protect him, I knew that if worse came to worse, I could save him, or at least let him get away, even if the creature chewed on me for a bit. More importantly, given the activity there, it was tangible; it was a place where even the insensitive said, "I don't like this place!" I knew someone like him, would pick right up on it. So all in all, I figured Coggers was it

I created for a long time a weekly rhythm I would do on Monday nights when I didn't have my children. I would get up at 5:00 a.m., go to my job, work like an asshole all day, come home and sleep for an hour or two then I would go and teach Chris. Usually we finished about 11:00 p.m. or so, I would drop him off and smudge, go to bed and be up at 5:00 a.m. again.

Is it any wonder that I could and can sleep anywhere?

So the next time we got together, we started a routine that lasts to this day. We would meet, go to Starbucks and he would get mocha and me a white chocolate fattening thing. Then we headed to my parents and walked over to the Training School, since I knew it would be perfect to get him in touch with energy. Chris was gung ho, even after the previous visions of someone running at us screaming, he was into it. Just walking up the main road to the Training School is a lesson. There are so many energy shifts there, it's amazing. As you walk up, you get hit with layers of creepiness, strong, palatable waves. I think even the most obtuse person would sense something at the Training School if they took a moment to attune to it. I also needed some time to prepare, seriously, I was a little leery of taking him to the woods. Let me say right now that I had been trying to get the Shamans down there for a year. I had told them, "Listen, this place isn't "I think, I sense, I feel." When it goes off, you're going to be saying, what the fuck is that? It doesn't go off every time you're there, maybe once or twice a year. Let's go."

No one did.

As we walked up and around the perimeter roads of the school, we talked about energy and how it gets infused into the area that surrounds it. How you could tap into it and feel it once you are aware of it. Yet, it carries a curse, because once you become aware, you're always aware. We walked and felt and sensed as I explained energy like this, "If you always go to one room when you're mad and just sit in there and feel angry, well, after a year or so, no one is going to feel good whenever they go and sit in that room." The Training School was like that, except worse. Thousands of kids had been sent there against their will. Thousands of children, feeling afraid, lost, scared, beat up. And while I know there were some happy times there, for the most part, everything I had heard was horrible.

We felt it.

When we went down to Cogs, as soon as we walked up the hill, I could feel shifts in the energy. I can't describe it better than this. You take a step and the air feels different, sometimes lighter, as in you feel good, in this case, heavier, as in it feels crappy, somewhat dirty. Since we were tuned into it from the Training School, Chris could feel it as well. As soon as you left the asphalt and stepped into the woods, you could feel it. It's subtle, but there. As we headed down the hill I took a good look at my new friend, to reassure myself he was going to make it. Its ok for me, I know I could take care of myself, but to take him there was a different story. I had seen too many times what happens to people when they get afraid. So I was a little hesitant, as gifted as he innately was, this was still pretty heavy energy we are talking about. Lord help us if the Coggers creature came out to eat. We reached the bottom to be greeted by a tranquil scene of the moon being reflected over the water. Coggers was a beautiful place at night, and it still is, even now with most of it gone. The bullfrogs croaking, the occasional splash of a bass on the surface, if you didn't know any better, you would think it was just another New England pond.

I knew better.

We planted our butts in the sand and I exhaled a deep breath, feeling that inner calm that I had discovered. We spent an hour or so, just sensing the spirits around us, listening to them walk around, seeing the occasional person standing there. Seriously that's what it was, someone standing there. We've all seen dark shadows out of the corners of our eyes (see my next book) well, this was seeing people, or part of people, literally, standing there. I don't know how many times his head whipped around. "There was someone right there!" I can tell you, either the number of spirits had quintupled or I had become a lot more aware of them, because they were all around us. We could hear footsteps, and the gravel crunching behind us. Chris kept looking around. "What's that?" and he turned completely around to sit facing that direction. I said to him, "Dude, it doesn't matter if a whole horde of demons come running down that hill at us if you're in the right space." And it's true. If you are in the right place, feeling connected, feeling love, nothing dark can affect you. I had seen that time and time again, feeling God's presence in everything and trusting in the purpose of life,(which shields you like you wouldn't believe). I didn't even have to consciously act that way, it was just a part of who I was. With Susan, it was so simple she couldn't accept it. Love is the opposite of fear, it's the opposite of any negative emotion. I had seen in the house in Georgetown, and I had felt it in my own heart. Crappy stuff can't stand love. So as long as I felt connected and inner peace, I could have had a demon dancing on my head and it wouldn't bother me, more importantly, it wouldn't want to even be near me.

Hey, you can sit there and mentally project all sorts of things. You can spend hundreds or thousands of dollars taking classes about psychic protection. The deal is, be at peace, be happy and connected - that's it! As I see it, that's what so many of us Americans lack,(of course without taking pills),in our society, muff" said.

So we sat down there for an hour or so, just enjoying the night and seeing what we could sense. We kept hearing footsteps and a few times we heard a metal ringing noise, almost like sonar. I wish I could convey the scene better to you, sitting there, looking at my new friend in the grey moonlight, trying to calm him down from the crazy noises around us. After a while we joined hands and ran energy together. We called it a night and went back to my house where we smudged each other.

That first visit always sticks in my mind, the moonlight, the ringing noises, just the simple pretty New England night.

Meteaching and him being completely open to what I had to say. Also seeing him realize, "Yes, it was like Norman said, there is a world all around us." We were just sitting in the woods that night, laughing and talking then all of sudden feeling afraid and wanting to run out of there, getting rid of it through grounding, then laughing again. Over and over, feeling some horrible things and visualizing even worse, then bringing myself back to that good place inside. Not letting the energy affect me, or trying not to. I also had an innate fear of the woods that interfered. This was a place that my friends and I got the crap scared out of us, many times. It was only my faith and love that was able to make me face the things that had chased me out as a kid.

After the second time we went to Coggers, I decided to bring a tape recorder with me. I had heard of EVPs, (Electronic Voice Phenomena), way back at the Mansion when someone was speaking there about them. It was an interesting phenomena, because it was supposed to represent spirit communication. Think of it this way, if you and I are sitting at a table, and we have a tape recorder between us, and we hear a third voice, who's speaking? Now, if the voice is responding to what we are talking about, isn't that even further proof that there is something interacting with us that we aren't aware of. I had gotten a couple of recordings with the Shamans during investigations with them using my crappy reel to reel hand held recorder. So I decided to give it a shot at Coggers, plus, I really wanted to record that weird metal sonar noise we kept hearing. So we did the usual, stopped at Starbucks, got some liquid candy and took a walk over to the Training School.

Though it might sound boring or the same by me saying, "we did the usual, "you have to understand that as sensitive's, while there, we would get assailed by emotions and energy. It was overwhelming at times, tough, but worth it. We always felt something, usually what Chris called, "that's orrible."

When we got down at the bottom of the hill, it was another beautiful night. I swear, every time I am there, I think, "this place is so pretty." The moon was out and I just felt so relaxed to be sitting there, instead of in my truck driving, or dealing with customers on the phone. Here I was with a friend, who had an interest in the spirit world like me, and I felt confident in my abilities to protect us both. Since I love the sound of my own voice and I love teaching, it was great to be there with someone who was open to learn. We spent a couple hours down there and at one point I remember feeling a spirit walk up right behind me, indeed, I felt my shirt get pushed in as it walked into me completely. I told Chris, "Something just walked into me, I could push it away if I wanted to, but I won't, because by it being in my energy field, trying to feed from it, I can learn more about the spirit."

He said, "Oh yeah, I'm familiar with that, I used to push them away just like this."

He put his left hand on his solar plexus, and his right hand out in front of him, palm up. Since the solar plexus is the third chakra which relates to your will power, it makes sense, using your will power to push something away. We could hear what sounded like people walking about on the paths above us and we heard that metal bonging noise a few times as well. I was all excited about what we might get on recorder when I realized that the tape had run out!!!

UGH!

Well, even if it had run out, at least we recorded for awhile. At the end of the night when we held hands and ranenergy, creating sacred space, we heard footsteps all about us. We rushed back to my place and started listening to the recorder. Even though it was 11 o'clock at this point and I was tired, we both wanted to hear if we got anything. When we got to the part where Chris said, "I used to push them away like this," we heard a voice, clear as day say, "Don't touch me."

Whoa, what the fuck. It was so clear that we could hear it over the crappy, "whhrrr whrrrr" of the reels. It sounded as clear as our voices, just a little faint. We went through the whole tape, sitting in my truck in my driveway, till it was about 12:30 or so. Boy, was I tired. We captured that odd metal noise on the tape as well. I was kind of bummed out that the tape recorder had run out before we left because it was really active near the end of the night. I know we would have gotten more if we had been recording.

BUT WE HAD GOTTEN PROOF.

Proof that what we were feeling was real and not something we had imagined. Here was proof that the spirit world isn't some ghostly shade, repeating the same thing over and over, but that it interacted with us. This was huge. I spent the whole week telling my friends about it, hell even if you didn't believe in the spirit world, and you knew me, chances were at one point I shoved a recorder in your face and played it for you. To me, it was very cool stuff.

The following week, we got my friend Dave to go with us. We were at the bottom of the hill, talking and laughing and feeling spirits. I felt so calm, so collected, the exact opposite of the guy I had been the last five years. I sat down and started meditating. When I felt I had gathered all my energy up around me, I shot it out saying, "It's me!" Those woods knew me. I had played in them, and whatever spirits were down there, they had seen all my triumphs and tribulations. That place knew me and here I was casting my energy into it, saying, "Here I am mother fucker, come get me." And then I looked at Dave and Chris and said, "Wait about a half hour, then it will get weird down here," and that brings us full circle in this tale. It was then that the thing that had scared the hell out me and any friends as kids came out and challenged us. That's what it was you know, a challenge, it challenged what we were and what we stood for. This thing, (that my brother and I called the "Coggers creature"), came out from wherever it was, or transformed from the energy that it was and materialized and tried to scare us. I am pretty sure that it had grown fat and bloated with energy from the number of times it had scared the hell out of my friends and I as kids and all the other people, whose stories I don't know to this day. It came out and tried to frighten us away. Dave was in the zone, that's all I can say. Whether or not you can tell from the recording, for about 40 seconds, I reverted back to that scared little kid who had been chased out of the woods all those times. My first thought was, "Holy fuck, its here!"

      Isn't that the way with our childhood demons? Don't they usually grow larger in our mind's eye and take on more power? Well, I knew this thing, and it knew me, and from growing larger to me, with my knowledge, it had grown smaller. Now, here it was shrieking at us, from ten feet away, and I remembered in that moment, all the times I had ran for my life. Thank God for Dave. While I was mentally remembering everything that had happened to me, he was welcoming it, without fear, without anything but love in his heart. The exact opposite from what **It** wanted from us. Honest to God, as it was sitting there shrieking, behind us the beaver was slapping its tail on the water's surface, so that it was a constant distraction. As we looked at the top of the hill, we could see the headlights of a car on the street, lighting up the top of the hilltop. The spirit went, "reah reah," and my head whipped around and stared at the spot it came from, then the beaver slapped its tail and I turned towards that, and the spirit went, "reahreah," so it became almost like something out of Laurel and Hardy. Chris pointed out to me, "Look dude," and those lights from the hilltop had spread farther down the path, so that it looked like a car was in someone's backyard lighting up the woods, and the beaver slapped its tail and the spirit screamed, "reahreah." I told Dave afterwards, how perfect he was, "If an oily black tentacle had uncoiled from the bushes, you would have shaken hands with it."

My recorder was being used by the Shamans at the time. We were using Dave's, and his reel to reel only worked on noise activation, there wasn't a continuous record setting. So the whole time this thing is shrieking at us, I kept having to activate it. I kept whistling to get the reels turning again because whatever the Cooger's creature was, it wasn't registering on the recorder. So imagine me, facing the terror of my childhood, hearing it yell at me from ten feet away, turning when the beaver slapped its tail, to make sure something else wasn't going to try and eat us, looking at the lights on top of the hill and checking the recorder. Thankfully we got most of it, and if you've made it this far, and listened to that file, I am sure you can tell it doesn't sound like it came to chat about tax laws, whatever it was, it was mad. After it ran to the other side of the pond, we talked about it for awhile and stayed down there another hour or so. Later on, we ran crazy energy, stronger than I think I have ever felt since. Give it another listen. **PLAY REAH EVP**

Here's what I think about EVPs and how they work. The human hearing range is roughly from 20 to 20,000 hertz, a dog's is 67- 65000 hertz, and hopefully as you know, a hertz is how they measure sound, in cycles of energy. This simple fact explains how dogs can hear a dog whistle while we are oblivious to it, the dog whistle is at a higher frequency than we can hear. Indeed, a recorder picks up from 10 to 70,000 hertz, (the good ones) and becausespirits are typically out of our hearing range, we won't notice them, but the recorder can. Now think of a spirit, its frequency is so much higher than humans. It's pure energy and not weighted down by the McDonald's that it had for lunch, wondering if can make it to the bathroom in time. Well, a spirit doesn't have a voice box or a trachea, but what is sound? It's a wave. What is a sound wave? Ultimately everything is some form of energy, so sometimes when a spirit is powerful enough, it can use enough energy to create a sound wave and make itself heard in our dimension. As in the recording at the beginning of the book, that spirit had so much energy it could punch through into our dimension and make itself known. More often than not, sprits use existing sound waves, via voices or noises to tag its message along. I have over 400+ EVPs where a spirit talks among us, or overrides my voice. So that you might hear, tap, tap and then an EVP or a voice so distinctly among mine that you can't make out what either of us are saying.

      The following week, you know Dave, Chris and I were down there, with shit-eating grins and high expectations, hoping for the Coggers creature to come out again. Dave and I had seen some cool stuff with the Shamans, but no one, no one that I knew of, (as adults), had experienced what we did that night. Whatever it was, we had beaten it. It didn't make us run away, or scream and cry for help, we had stood our ground and it ran off. For me, this was gigantic. How many times had I run crying out of the woods? How many times had I been afraid? I can't even begin to guess. Well, no more, we had held our space of inner peace, and it had driven it away. It reconfirmed what I had seen in that living room in Georgetown, dark spirits don't like light, they can't stand it. For the first time I had ever heard of, someone had defeated the, "Coggers creature" More importantly, I wanted to get it on recorder again. I had seen the limit of reel-to-reel recording and the damn tape kept running out week after week. The thought of getting more tapes never seemed to cross my mind, so I went and spent some coin on a really nice digital recorder. I was so excited to be using it, I even read the little manual that comes with it, you know, the ones we usually throw away.

So down at the bottom of the hill again, it was a heavy night, (meaning we really felt the spirits), and we could hear all sorts of stuff around us, and sensed even more. I cannot express that about the woods, it's really overwhelming. Usually in investigations with the Shamans we would go to a haunted house, then speak with the owners finding out where it was the worst. Then we would go into a haunted room or a haunted hallway and try and sense if we felt any presences there. Well, in Coggers, you were surrounded by spirits and when you were trying to tap into one, another one was punching you in the back of the head and even another was dancing in front of you. That's what made the recorder so good, it might get what we would miss. That night, across the pond, we all heard something scream. To me, it sounded like a woman, to Chris, a cat and to Dave, it sounded like a crow. How the hell can you all hear something and it sound different to all of us? It was another case of Andy and I, or when Katrina and I were in the woods, what sounded like a helicopter to me sounded like demonic laughter to her. Why? How? Well, it's simple. Our brains are really just giant receivers. Everything you think we know about the brain is wrong. There aren't areas that are labeled memory or instinct; that's old science. Since the 1950's and Karl Pribram's experiments, we have learned that our brains really act like radio stations for all the waves of information we are bombarded with.

Our brains receive the information waves, (light, sound, etc., etc.), and creates our world around us. Let me give you an example that will aggravate any PETA fans that happen to be reading this. Karl Pribram did an experiment where they cut almost all the optic nerves of cats, yet the cat could still see and do its thing, unhindered. Now, if the traditional, "your eyes project an image onto your brain, "beliefs were used, that would be like watching a movie with a busted projector, yet still watching the whole movie. Well, that wasn't the case, the cat could move and dance and do its cat thing. So even with bad eyes, the cats still saw ok.

In the 1930's, Schmidt did experiments with the brains of rats, trying to find the location of memory. He would teach a rat how to get through a maze, and then burn a part of its brain, trying to find the location. If he burned the memory part, the rat wouldn't be able to figure out the maze after he put the brain back in. Guess what, he burned every part of the rat's brain and the rat could still do the maze. No part of a rat's brains were related to memory and this has been reconfirmed by other experiments, our image of the brain is completely wrong. Now back to the eyes. The current belief is that our eyes receive the wavelengths of light and our brain processes it and creates a 3D environment around us. So we all do perceive the world differently, each in our own unique way. Can you understand how amazing that is ? How it reaffirms all the teachings of, "you are unique and special in the whole universe." Nothing and no one see's the world as you do, if that doesn't cheer you up on a bad day, I don't know what will .How many times has a friend pointed out a member said, "Wow, look at them! They are so hot!" and you've thought to yourself, "What the hell are they talking about? That person is gross." Well to them, that person is attractive, because purpose has decided they need to be and wants them to connect, yet you see them as they truly are. Trust me, I have amazing women flirt with me all the time, and I know what I see in the mirror.

Whatever screamed that night in Coggers, it just busted right through the dimensional barrier and it sounded unique to each of us. Even the previous week, to Dave, he said it sounded like a crow, to me, well, I just kept thinking that "it" was here.
PLAY HEY CAT EVP

Close your eyes and imagine sitting next to a pond, it's a nice cool night, you can hear bass jumping and crickets chirping. The breeze caresses your face and from the shrubs behind you, you hear movement, like an animal is there, but when you look, nothing. You hear leaves move, but not just a rustle, but a sustained movement for a minute or more, just in one spot. While you're sitting there trying not to pay attention to it, (and give it energy), you hear a footstep behind you, or feel the tingles run down the left side of your body as a spirit walks into to you. That's what I mean by Cogger's and how it had heavy energy. If we were in a house, I have no doubt that dolls with glowing red eyes would be running around with their heads doing 360's, shooting green vomit in streams at us. It was that strong down there. Later on, when we were running energy, three grown men, holding hands next to the pond, trying to feel love,(again, I'm not gay), we all felt spirits walking into us. While standing there, remembering the good things and feeling my heart open, all of a sudden, I would feel sad, or afraid. Then I would go back to my heart, and think, "It's ok," cause that's what Dave and I were taught and that's what we were teaching Chris, that's it's ok to feel these things, but move them, and get rid of it. It's ok to feel sad, but not forever. How many people do you know cling to the past like that? My ex-wife is still mad about things that I said 10 years ago. Well, let it go! It is time to move on. Certainly once you're stuck on the other side, it's harder to change those emotions, so we would feel the energy and we let them go.

That's what we were doing, changing those emotions or trying too.

That's healing. Think of it. Your friend complains to you, you listen and open your heart and remind them that it's ok to feel what they feel. That changes it for them and they love talking to you.

That's healing.

When we got done and were talking about what we had sensed, I felt some huge chills that made me shudder and go, "Wahh," (later on when I played back the EVPs there was a very lovely "AHAHHAHAHA" voice). Listening to that afterwards, it made me question what I was sensing. **PLAY HAHAHA and CHILLS EVP**. We all walked away feeling a little amazed and humbled by what we had felt. We went back to my house for smudging, and while doing so we all stopped and saw a black shadow, in motion.

Seriously, each of us looked at each other and I said, "Did you just fucking see that?" I laughed it off because my house was already haunted, but I realized we were bringing spirits out of the woods, home with us.

Great.

That week I started a process that I follow to this day. I went in and even though it was late, I burned those recorder files to CDs. The next day I put the disks in my pickup, and while I drove across the face of the planet, spreading the joy of decorative concrete around the earth, I listened to them. The difference on what we picked up from tape to digital was amazing. I mean, forget about the, "Whir whir," noise of the reel to reel, but the range of EVPs. Previously, we had gotten like two or three, now we got hundreds. In fact, that day I went and bought a little notebook that I could keep with me to write down what I heard. If you ever came across me driving across the state in those years, it was with a notebook and pen on my lap, barely paying attention to the road. I was constantly rewinding and re-listening to files, with the stereo cranked to the max. I am, to this day, amazed I didn't kill anyone. I will always remember that first day listening to them. I was sitting in my truck, in the rain, in someone's backyard, listening to the EVPs instead of working. Hearing me tell a childhood story about Cogs and hear a spirit confirm part of it, and I realized there was something in the truck with me. I knew if I had my recorder going I would've gotten more EVPs, I knew it! I could feel it, feel the darkness, the presence, and stupid me, wishing I had a recorder with me, instead of trying to clear it. I can't tell you how draining it was, to hear that, to feel that with me, it was like Coggerswas saying, "Hey asshole, like to come play with us? Let's hang out with you and see how you feel!"

Still, I was elated we got so many EVPs that first night. So many of them, that any of the "supposed" ghostshows on TV would've been green with envy if they heard what we had recorded. The three of us that night got two names, Bobbi and Vincent, which was a first. Bobbi who? Vincent who? We also recorded a kind of request for help. It kind of sounds like a Scotsman, "get us oot!"**PLAY BOBBI EVP, PLAY GET US OOT**

I think after that I was instantly addicted and so was Chris. He and I started going down there every other week, always bringing the digital recorder, always being aware of what was around us, and always appreciating the beauty of the place. Every time I went, I would think, "Wow, it's so pretty down here." Each time, we would get a ton of EVPs and then I would spend the next three days listening to them. Sometimes I would hear the clearest EVPs and get the chills and say, "Holy fuck." I would call him and excitedly tell him, "Dude, you won't believe what we got last night." After our night of playing with the spirit world in Coggers woods, the next day or two, as I listened through the files, I would feel beat up and tired, psychically tired. Like I took the SATs and someone was punching me in the brain the whole time. The days following I would always be sleepy and cranky and it would be hard for me to pull myself out of the funk. But another part of me was addicted, here was freaking proof that the place was haunted, here were spirits saying crazy things and we were recording it. All my experiences as a child were being validated. Everything I had thought and sensed was there, with what to me, was proof. It was fantastic because all of these EVPs just served to confirm what we felt, and we felt some crazy stuff. It was the exact opposite of the Shamans, which was, "Let's just wing it."

 And,

 "Oh, I channeled Jesus today."

 And,

 "Oh, that's a demon there."

 Hell, if they were there when the Coggers creature came, I think a couple of the Shamans would've run.

 One night Chris told me he had seen a spirit. He was amazed, "Lioke, I just sah someone standing there, looking at us." Later, as we stood there in the moonlight running energy, I actually saw a face over his. I am looking at Chris and all if sudden I see a face with a beard looking at me. I told him what I saw, and we both agreed, "Cool." It was cool because we were like kids playing with dynamite and each time it went off, somehow we would still have all our parts attached. After feeling and running energy and me lecturing him about what he was picking up, we would go back to my house and smudge each other. To be perfectly honest, some nights I would go to bed and know there was someone staring at me, standing at the foot of my bed and staring. Seriously, even as chronically exhausted as I was, it was kind of hard to fall asleep sometimes. My days of sensing a spirit and being afraid were over, but still, it was disconcerting.

I think it was our third trip down there that he said, "I don't have to worry about picking up a spirit, you will just take it off of me." I was aggravated because of the psychic hammering I was getting for him was wearing on me. I thought, "Ok man, time to step it up." That was part of the clearing process that I would do. Let him feel a spirit attach, feel that neck pain, go from good mood to crappy and then take it off. All this so that he could learn what it was like for a spirit to hang around him for a bit, but not send the spirits home with him so they'd be watchinghim eat breakfast, as they did to me. That week I told him, "Ok, get yourself in a happy place, cause this one is going home with you and you have to figure out how to get rid of it."

His open mouthed expression was priceless. "Close your mouth dude, you're attracting flies."

It really was such a great period of learning for both of us, and each time we went down, we would get more EVPs. Each batch of EVPs would have something unique about it. Maybe a name, maybe a loud noise that we didn't hear, something, and it kept drawing us back. No matter how tired and crappy I felt after work, Chris could always talk me into going down there. It was also during one drizzly night there, that I learned one of the most important lessons about EVPs. Mainly, if you sit there like a moron and ask spirits to, "Speak into the red light," they will ignore you, especially down Coggers. If you ask questions, you get shit for answers and out of the thousands of questions I've asked down there, I think I've only gotten one direct answer. BUT, they do respond when you say something that's worth them commenting on. Chris said "It's like being with a bunch of strangers at a coffee shop. If they hear you and feel the need to respond, they will, if not, they don't." I think it's because of the energy it takes for them to communicate with us. So I learned that while we talked about Monty Python for an hour or so, giggling and laughing, we didn't get one single EVP. Yet, I noticed we got a slew of EVPs when we talked about the afterlife. In later visits when I felt like it was slow, I would start talking about God and spirits, and we would get EVPs. In fact, when I took disbelievers in the spirit world down there, it was a way to be sure we got some. I also noticed during this period was that some spirits needed noise to speak. In some instances when listening to the file, you would hear a knock and a tap and a, "Bobby," or a water drop noise, a tap and a, "Boo," (and trust me, we did get "Boo's"). Sometimes the EVP would override our voices, and when listening, you would hear a third voice mixed in with ours. It's interesting and it made me think about the different types of spirits that we had communicating with us. Yet, not all EVPs were like that. Sometimes the spirit would come across clear as day, and skeptics refused to believe it was a spirit. Only by hearing the whole file did you realize that clear male voice only joined in our conversation once, or that there were only two of us there, not four or five, as the files suggested. We never knew what to expect and we never knew what we would get and that made me want to go more and more.

All in all, what I recorded and heard, (and how we got it), really changed the way I thought of the spirit world and investigations as a whole. A lot of it ran counter to what we had been taught by the Shamans. I had been told that spirits couldn't see one another, well, I got EVPs that told me they could. I had been told that spirits couldn't work off their emotions and needed help, well, guess what? Yep, you guessed it, some files ran counter to that line of thought.

Just the recordings themselves taught me so much about the spirit world and how it interacted with us. I mean some people go to investigations acting serious and walking around. Sensing this and feeling that, holding out recorders, hoping for a spirit to talk to them. Well, I had learned that it didn't matter what you did, if the spirit world wanted to talk to you, it was going to. Even more interestingly, if you had something worth commenting on, they would. So instead of sitting in a spot being quiet, we should be chatting away. Standing there, feeling and trying to be cool, investigators had the opposite effect. How egotistic is it to expect something to react the way you want it to? It's like watching a deer and expecting it to eat grass, lift a hind leg, drop a deer surprise and run off. Yes, these things might happen, but reality is, you're more of a jerk for expecting it to, (Yes, I just called you a jerk if you're that kind of person). Look at it from their point of view. If it took you power to communicate with someone just to say, "Hey," Would you do it to a bunch of knuckleheads acting all important and asking questions? Or would you be like you were in life? Reacting and commenting on things worth commenting on. There are so many EVPs of them laughing or calling me an idiot, and only one of them answering a direct question from me. Any surprise that shows like, "Ghost Hunters," or, "Taps," or any of the other lame ass TV programs out there get few good EVPs?

Let me say this right off. If you have to do anything to the recordings, to make them heard. Those are not EVPs. Those are odd noises that you've messed with to the point that it sounds like something. An EVP is heard without having to play it backwards, or clear it up. Screwing with the data makes it a sound effect. I can record myself farting and play with the file to the point where it comes across as, "The other side is scary!" That's not an EVP, that's Hollywood.

Back to our story.

Chris was becoming a great friend who listened to my stories and lessons intently, and shared great insights of his own that would often make me pause. I started learning from him in return, and that's what I think it's about. My old teacher would never ask for advice and thought he knew everything. I used to say to him, "Dude, you're not God." With Chris, it was a give and take that continues to this day and through teaching him, I learned. I mean, we are all gifted, all of us, each in our own way, we have things to offer and teach. You can do things I would never be able to dream of doing, and vice versa. So instead of being jealous of each other's gifts, (the fact that you can levitate objects while I can control dust), we should honor each other for our path in life and light. Given all the EVPs I was getting, and the things I was learning from them, that's not what I was receiving from the Shamans. Some real problems started developing there, between all of us, that came to a head.

CHAPTER 14

So while I was going down to Coggers with Chris and teaching him, some cracks started appearing in my friendship with the Shamans. As I got to know them individually, I saw that far from being perfect, (who is?), they were just like me, flawed, weak and petty. As I learned from them and began having my own experiences, I encountered a lot of jealousy.

Please understand, here I was, someone who had come back from the darkness. I was a Reiki Master and had been healed by the divine. From being a whiny person that drove everyone away, I was actively being sought out by people, for help. I felt a sense of pride, in some respects, for the first time in years. So when I told a Shaman about something that I did to help someone, I didn't want them to be threatened by it, all I wanted was a simple, "Good job dude." That's not what I got. I couldn't mention doing anything for anyone without hearing, "I had this healing the other day and it was amazing," or "Well, I did this," in return. It was like no one wanted to be outdone by the other. It really bothered me, in part because it was just so much hypocrisy. For someone to say to me, "So and so just wants attention, look at them!" Then join hands 20 minutes later in a circle and be able to hold so much love in their heart to cross a spirit, well, that didn't ring true.

Remember, I am a concrete worker, I am all for seeing is believing.

Give me months of this type of gossip within and about each other and pretty soon my hobby is exactly like my day job. Aggravating. I was and will spend the rest of my days working off my ego. That statement alone is filled with ego! Well, the Shamans were just one big pile of it. I guess I would say I stopped feeling the openness and love that drew me to them.

I started having issues with the head Shaman as well. I found that while he was so gifted, it felt like he was looking for people to fawn over him. I used to call his students, "bobbleheads," because I think if he had said, "My left toe was once used by the Pope to heal the Red Sea, "somepeople would've agreed with him. I would often question things and get dirty looks in return. I was amazed by him. He was and is an intensely powerful man, but I also wanted to learn and feel on my own. Come on, I was teaching someone now, I just didn't want to be his mouthpiece like the others. That's what I felt it was too, everyone just kind of regurgitating what he had taught us, instead of developing their own guidance.

My impatience with him and he with me started showing in investigations too,. Every time we went into a house, we would meet the people and talk to them for an hour or so. Explaining the spirit world and how it reacts to us. Well, after hearing the same stories 15 times, and merely being a silent person standing there, nodding my head, I started getting frustrated. What we felt in houses was nothing in comparison to

Coggers. I would listen impatiently for a bit then I would interrupt and ask, "What's the scariest part of your house?" After they told me, I would look at the group and say, "I'm going to sit there in the dark for awhile, and see what I get," and walk away rudely. Bear in mind, usually I had to get a sitter for the kids while I was doing this, so I hated wasting time. It got to the point that he wouldn't ask my opinion or ask after we were done.

Yes, I realize that this sounds whiny, but remember, this is coming from a man who was supposed to be my teacher and friend, and who was all about making you feel special. I have to admit, my ego was bruised.

Not one time did it ever occur to me that the woods had anything to do with my attitude. It never crossed my mind. I know now that I had things attached like leeches to me, but then, all I knew was they weren't very spiritual. I didn't see how people could pretend to hold so much love that they created a doorway between dimensions, yet be petty and spiteful. Eventually it came to a breaking point when I was walking around in the woods with them, looking for alien landing sites in the area. Here I was, paying someone to watch my children, so I could go out and learn with the Shamans, and we are in the woods looking for aliens?

I don't think so.

Well, reality was, I doubted a lot of what they sensed. When they felt a cold spot, they would say, "There is a demon there!" Having had cold spots dance on my brain for hours on end, I really didn't think so. When we said a prayer together and they channeled angels, I was asking myself, "I wonder what is pretending to be an angel?" Reality is, I had someone who wanted to learn what I knew and I had the most haunted place in America to visit, I was done with the Shamans.

CHAPTER 15

A couple of weeks after I left the group, maybe about three or four months from the first time I had taken Chris under my wing, we had plans to go down there again. I must be honest, I didn't want to. The sustained psychic drain was starting to take its toll on me, and I wasn't meditating enough to replace the energy I was losing. When you throw in my departure with the Shamans, well, I wasn't in the best of moods to be heading down there and running light and love. Add to that mix, being a single dad, working 900 hours a week and listening to EVPs full time, I was whipped. I called my friend Pat and she decided to come down there. Part of me felt relieved because she is a very powerful woman and could take some of the load off, to help me if the Coggers Creature decided to come out. It was starting to get cold, so Chris and I started a fire. Few things are better than having a fire at night next to a pond, with a good friend. I got to show off my fire making skills that I had learned as a misspent youth in Coggers! **PLAY LIGHT THE FIRE** When Pat finally made it, (my directions had gotten her lost), we had even more fun. She has a great easy laugh, which I am always trying to take advantage of. She's a great woman with a big heart and a wonderful sense of humor. We spent a fun night down there, laughing and talking, and we got an amazing assortment of

EVPs. Pat, being the cool woman that she is, had brought me a huge bag of smudge, and while sitting there, I threw some on the fire. We got an EVP that sounds like it says, "Hurts to."It's faint and hard to make out, but still interesting when you think that smudge is supposed to get rid of spirits! For the first time I recorded a high pitched female voice giving us a name. We also got an EVP after I told her that we had crossed some spirits the week before, it said, "Bullshit," **PLAY BULLSHIT EVP** which really made me think about what we were doing. Later, when we started running out of firewood, we ran energy and put out the fire. Pat didn't want to accompany us down the path and headed home.

Since very little was left of the paths that I used to walk as a kid, Chris and I would sometimes walk around a bit and explore the remnants of Coggers in the dark. One night I saw my only full blown apparition and got a creepy EVP from it, which to me, confirmed what I had seen. I was walking along and all of sudden I saw a man in a flannel shirt standing there staring at me. When I blinked, it was gone. I walked up and asked questions, holding out the recorder in front of me, and personally, I got some nice creepy chills. I got very little on the EVP front, other than some creepy laughter at my chills. Well since then, Chris and I had made that area a regular stop. So that night he and I were there, running energy, we heard the leaves start to rustle behind us. At first we thought it was a breeze. When they kept rustling, and for some reason didn't stop, we paid attention. They just stayed in one spot, rustling and moving. It was very disconcerting. You could see it, you could literally see them, moving and rustling in a circle about two feet across. And while we were looking at one spot, it started doing it in another place behind us, and we stared there too. Pretty soon we had four places around us, moving and rustling and we got an EVP of something saying, "May he rise up."**PLAY MAY HE RISE UP** What the hell!

That is the creepiest spoken EVP I have ever heard. If you played the file, well, you know it doesn't particularly sound like it wants a hug. I don't know who or what "he" is, and I don't want to know. Maybe it was talking about the Coggers creature, maybe it was talking about something darker, whatever it was, I get goose bumps every time I hear it asI hope you do too. As I listened and isolated the file, I also noticed we started getting some kind of language that I couldn't understand. "Karkakaga," but said with force, intention.**PLAY KARKAKARGA EVP**

If you and I are sitting down in Coggers, talking, with the recorder between us, the next day we can remember the conversation. Even a week later, we can somewhat remember it. Well, anything outside of that conversation could be considered an EVP. At Cogger's, we would get so many EVPs; names, bips, baps, comments, voices, some of them clear as day, others really faint, so faint they drove me nuts trying to hear them. Because honestly, it sounded like some serious conversations were taking place at times among the spirit world. Well unless you have done it, you cannot imagine the sheer frustration of playing something over and over and over and over.

> And over and over and over.
> and over and over and over
> and over, well, you get the idea
> And over and over

After awhile, you begin to place words where there are just sounds. If you hear two distinct sounds, but not clearly, it's very easy to think that it is a two syllable word, (most ghost shows). So I decided to focus on just what we could hear clearly. On a few of them I swear I could hear conversations going on between spirits. Some of them sounded minutes long and I was like, "Come ON!" Who wouldn't be? Who wouldn't want to listen to a two minute conversation between two spirits? Sometimes, it sounded like they were arguing, others like they were just speaking. I harassed technologically minded friends, I asked everyone I could think of, but no one knew of a way to boost a specific frequency of a recording. It was very frustrating, but also a big driving force behind my new addiction of going down there. I knew that one day I would get something amazing. Maybe get the Coggers Creature on digital so that I wouldn't have keep listening to the whir whir of the reel to reel recorder when I wanted to creep myself out. Maybe I would get a spirit to just talk about the afterlife, or say something to help me understand why Coggers was the way it was.

    All these EVPs confirmed what I knew about the place, and why I grew up there. It truly validated my beliefs about the woods. I knew Coggers was special, I knew there wasn't anything like it anywhere else that I had heard of or been to. It has been my good fortune to have experienced the spirit world my whole life, but out of all the haunted houses, buildings and lands I have been too, nothing was like the Cogs. I would watch other ghost shows or listen to other peoples EVPs and chuckle to myself, for all their equipment, they had nothing like what I was getting with just a cheap digital recorder. Each time I went down there, I would get more. Chris didn't have to twist my arm too hard to get me there, but sometimes I had to twist his.

    Playing the files back and listening to them, I began to realize something important. We weren't doing what we thought we were doing. Don't get me wrong, we were running energy, but ever since that time with Dave, Chris and I, when we heard that, "AHAHAHAHAH," afterwards, (that sounded so crappy) I knew something was up. That EVP told me whatever was behind me, it wasn't feeling the light and love I was running, itwas enjoying making me feel a chill. When you add the, "bullshit," EVP that we got when we were talking to Joy, about crossing spirits, well, something wasn't right, and I wanted to know what. I felt energy. I felt things walking into me and rushes of energy up to my heart and head. Obviously it wasn't what we had been taught it was. I had been told getting your heart open and cranking it, feeling that energy rush up to your crown,(the top of your head), was a spirit going to heaven. You were crossing it. Well, the EVPs were proving that to be wrong.

    I would tell people,"I will take one ounce of data over a thousand I think, I sense, I feels." Not realizing how rude I sounded at the time. All the EVPs were proving the "I think, I sense," wrong. I didn't think it was the energy; that was real, there was no denying it. I knew we were running energy. The spirits confirmed it over and over again via EVP. I knew energy was real. I had seen so many examples of it that it had to be. I thought it was the energy itself, what it was being used for, that was what I was confused about. Still, something was up. Spirits don't waste their power unless they think they are going to get something back. So for them to comment and say, "Bullshit," told me, well, it was bullshit. But why? Was it just me? Was it something else? The more I thought about crossing spirits, the more I started seeing the EGO of it all. Listen, I am a really great, modest guy. I am a Reiki Master, a Karuna Reiki Master and a Shamballa Master. I've also had the spirit world messing with me for years. I have seen truly amazing things that defy logic. I have and had worked with powerful people, but think about it for a moment. How egotistical is it of me to think that in a half hour I can come to your house, cross spirits, and clear the place? How egotistical is it to think that anyone in a 10 minute love fest, is going to heal something that a spirit has been feeling for years, because that's what I was taught. Hold hands, open your heart and get it cranking, get that love flowing from you and into each other, and you will open the door to the other side (heaven).

Trust me, I know how it sounds. It's true though, basically in a nutshell, that's what we were taught. Don't get me wrong. I am not knocking the power of love, or the power of running energy in circles. Remember, I was healed by the ultimate love and it made me open to everything, but really what were we doing? I knew from the faint, "healer," EVP that we were doing something good, but again, what? I began to examine what I was taught, and what I had learned from the Shamans. It really was eye opening. We all know that hindsight is 20/20, well, I started seeing perfectly. I started remembering all the times we had to return to a house and re-clear it. "The home owner is attracting more spirits." While I believe that to be true, that some people do attract spirits, I don't think it was the case in all the houses we went to, after re-clearing it, a few times we had to go back again, and again. I wonder about all the other times when we weren't called back, whether or not the people just got sick of seeing our smiling Moonie faces. After listening to the EVPs, I started doubting whether or not we were crossing spirits in the first place. In fact, it made me doubt a lot of things about the Shamans that I had been taught. This really opened up a dark chapter in my spiritual life, one that I will always fight, and continue to fight to this day. Remember also, Chris and I were going down there and rolling around and hugging the spirits there. That added to whatever other doubts I had been having and they fed from it. I had been calling myself a Shaman for over a year. Well, I looked up Shamanism online and got a couple of great books on it and guess what? I found I wasn't a Shaman and really, no one else I knew was too.

What I learned was this. Around the whole world there were 12 cultures that are labeled as Shamanic. All these cultures were completely disparate and had only one thing in common. It was called, "the ecstatic trance state," and basically they took a drug to induce themselves into a five or six hour meditative state, to get information or healing for whoever was coming to see them. In Siberia, where we get the word Shaman from, they took mushrooms. In South America, they took the Ayahuasca, a drink. The more I learned about it, the less sure I became, and certainly given my concrete background, the more opinionated I became about when other people were calling themselves Shamans. As I told a friend one day outside my apartment, the different cultures had different beliefs. The Koreans believed that only women could be Shamans. The South Americans believed that everyone was a Shaman with some more gifted then others. The Siberians, they believed that the spirits chose the Shamans, and that usually the people didn't want to become them because of the toll it took on them and their family.

Sound familiar? Anybody? Anybody? Bueller? Bueller?

Back to the ecstatic trance state, here's a good example. I am being bothered by an infectious boil on my back. I would go visit a Shaman and they would take the drug of the area and go into this trance, protected by helpers, and while the shaman was out of body, they would visit the spirit world and try to get them to leave me alone. Well, I didn't know one person who did this, and in fact, when I talked to the head Shaman about it, he told me, "If you've taken Ayahuasca in a past life, it's in your energy field, and therefore you can activate it whenever you need to."

Riigggghttt.

When I met people at spiritual groups and they said, "Oh, I am a Shaman, "I would go off on 10 minute tangents about Shamanism, about the ecstatic trance state and ask them, "How can you do that in a 30 minute session." Needless to say, I made few friends during that period.Ha-ha what a difference from being the open, kind and loving person I had been for the last year or so. Combine this attitude with going into the heaviest space in the area, with a lot of judgment, and well, I wasn't very open anymore. I began to wonder why people got on the spiritual path to begin with. I had seen so many in search of a name for themselves, (Shamans, Shamans) or money, (everybody everybody everybody). I met very few that had been drawn to it like me. Seriously, just to repeat myself for the 100th time, I was pulled on this path against my will. I never wanted to have anything to do with the spirit world, ever. Tell me what 12 year old kid wants to hear tapping coming from inside a one inch board thick wall that's level with his head? I never ever wanted to have anything to do with Coggers, other than the great fishing and fire building place it was. No, the spirit world clamored for my attention, because I was sensitive to it, because I believed in it. The more I believed in it, the more they clamored for my attention, a horrible scary catch 22. Now that I was on the path to understanding them, well, I was glad for it, humbled by it, but at the same time, hell no.

My conversations with Chris helped me through this a lot. He knew the Shamans and everyone else, so having him agree with me, helped validate my thoughts to myself. I also started telling people to stop calling me a Shaman. I realized I didn't deserve the title.

So, from being the open, kind hearted, loving person that the healing had made me, I started becoming a miserable scrooge for awhile. I would tease small helpless animals, and take candy from children. Ha-ha, no, but I did start to question everyone's motives in becoming spiritual. Instead of being open and loving to everyone and more importantly, un-judgmental, I looked at people with suspicious eyes. When someone told me of other healers and readers I thought to myself, "Bah, why are they doing this?"

Right around this time I started hearing spirits. While this might sound like a statement from someone who needs to get their head checked, it wasn't like I thought it would be. Much like seeing spirits, (I always imagined that seeing ghosts would be some guy with an 18th century derby and topcoat saying, "Hey chum, give us a hand here, eh?"), where all I saw was wispy energy. Hearing spirits was a quick, "Reh," or a low, "Uhgalahow." I think it was because I was so focused on listening to them by now, (almost every single day), that I began to attune myself to it. They sounded almost exactly like what I heard on the EVPs files 50 percent of the time. Just some sort of growl. Usually when I was in Cogger's, they would be confirmed by the EVPs themselves. I would hear something and ask if anyone else did, no one else would, and then when playing it back, hear it on the recording.

Very cool

I guess

Chris and I kept going to Coggers. As fall turned into winter, we went down dressed in heavier and heavier clothes. We started fires, and would sit there and talk about life, about spirituality, about everything under the sun. Always aware, always paying attention to what we felt. Sometimes it was really heavy, and we would strive to stay in the zone. Sometimes it was just nice out (but cold) and we would giggle and laugh most of the night. Down the path was a different story. It was always dense down there. Every time we stood across from each other and ran energy, those leaves would rustle and then move towards us, until eventually, there would be three or four spots about two or three feet in circumference rustling and moving. You could turn around and stare at them, and look, it wouldn't go away or stop, it would still rustle. It was a good test to open your heart and keep focused while listening to that right behind you.

One night Chris turned and said, "I don't think that's human," as he pointed to a rustling pile. "He's human,"**PLAY HE'S HUMAN EVP** was the reply that came clearly across. What did I learn from that? Besides the fact that it's a clear EVP, it also told me that spirits can see each other. This blew my mind and was the opposite of what I was taught. More importantly, by this time, I had two recorders. We got this same EVP on both recorders that were about five feet apart. Think about that for a moment. Instead of a spirit speaking at the recorder like everyone believed. It was a sound wave, much like your voice is. Seriously, that is amazing. **PLAY HE'S HUMAN RECORDER 2**

Another time, Chris said to me,"I am more afraid of people than of ghosts." I told him, "Don't call them ghosts, call them spirits." That moment we got an EVP that said,"Valiant!".**PLAY VALIANT EVP** How many years has it been since humans used the word valiant as an adverb? And I thought about it and realized "ghosts" was a generic term. No one wanted to have someone to say, "Look at that HUMAN over there." We like to be called people. Spirits seem to be the same way. Don't call them a ghost, call them spirits.

As winter came, we called a halt. It was just too damn cold to go and sit for hours in one place. Running energy, we would be shaking from the cold. Part of me said, "No way," with relief. Another part was a little sad. Given the quality and quantity of the EVPs we were getting, I really wanted to get some more, always more. I became like Warren Buffet or Bill Gates of EVPs from Coggers. Being with the Shamans, I had met the supposed EVP king of New England. When I sent him a file from Coggers, he was so amazed by what we had gotten he said, "Get me down there, you got to get me down there." Like a greedy kid I said, "No way."

If you look at the lights on the right side, and above the snow bank, you will see why this photo is in the book. I took this as a off the cuff shot. Blowing it up, reveals a large amorphous shape. When I say, "I see things" sometimes, this is what it looks like.

How much was enough?

I could never have enough EVPs, and part of me kept hoping that I would get that breakthrough EVP that would tell me everything everyone wanted to know about the afterlife.

I don't know why, I really don't, but I did think that one day we would. Not that they ever answered any questions or were helpful in any way at all in our quest to figure it out. No, quite the opposite, but I was hoping that they would slip and tell us, "We're here cause of the fire in 1812," or something.

One February day we got a break in the weather. We headed down to Cogs. We did a walk through a cemetery, and since it was still early and the cemetery didn't beat on our souls enough, we went for a walk through the Training School. It was a pretty dense night, and as usual, we were aware of the energy shifts as we walked up the road. When we got in back of all the buildings, it was even heavier for some reason. I had brought my camera and was busy taking snaps (as well as recording). I don't know what I was hoping for, maybe to get some spirits dancing or maybe just some orbs, but I remember we heard a scream, a long drawn out, "Ahhhhhhhhhhh," off in the distance. Other than looking at each other and saying," Didya hear that?" It drew no more attention, (screams being pretty much a commonplace occurrence by now). When we were walking down the road that made our circuitous loop, it really felt heavy. Our hearts hurt, and we both commented on it. As we drew closer to Princeton Boulevard, we suddenly smelled shit. Yes, shit. It was so strong, a septic nasty smell, and Chris asked, "What the hell is that?" I replied, "It's the opposite of love, it's the energy that feeds on hate, fear, anger, it can't stand love, compassion, honor and happiness." The smell quickly went away, and we continued on down Princeton Boulevard and did the loop into Coggers from Cashin Street.

When I played those EVPs back and downloaded those pictures, holy crap! There were two amazing photos. One showed a wispy white stream of smoke in front of the Training School buildings. It actually looked like how I see spirits. The other was a whitish blue orb, (that I took in back), when you zoomed in on it, you could clearly see a smiling face. We got the usual assortment of joy from the EVPs, none very clear, but a lot of "reh" and grunts.

I spent most of that winter meditating and relaxing. Chris and I talked often. I took another class with Susan and ended up becoming a Karuna Reiki master as well. The more I developed energy modalities, the more in tune I felt, and the more I felt drawn to the spirit world. I would notice more and see more. Coggers kept calling me, and I couldn't wait till the weather turned and we could go back down there. I had played some EVPs for friends, and got them interested as well.

One day during meditation I asked myself when it would be most active for us to return, (since you never really knew when the Coggers creature would come out). Well, I heard pretty clearly a date. So, I made some calls and I went down there with Chris, Dave and another person who was gifted, who I knew could see spirits. Per usual, we sat at the bottom of the hill, talking and laughing like always and that night, we got amazing EVPs. When I was talking about the fire spot at the top of Brownie Hill and wondering out loud who built it, I heard "MARY MENKHAM". **PLAY MARY MENKHAM EVP** After a couple hours, we walked down the path and ran energy there, and it got really crazy. Behind each of us, the leaves were rustling per usual, but this time it felt even denser, worse somehow. My friend kept glancing at them and said, "Those are MICE....MICE!"

"Sorry, but mice tend to run away from people, not towards them, and there's not 100 mice under those leaves moving around together, or that one, or that one," I replied as I pointed to where the leaves were rustling.

She was kind of freaked out, although I wasn't surprised. It is spooky to see things moving without reason. What surprised me was her vehemence. I think it made her doubt her talents. Her and I had both seen things and pointed at the same spot,"There's something right there," a slew of times. I knew she could see spirits better than I from our discussions. Yet she couldn't see these things down here, and neither could I. Why???? To this day, I don't know, but I would hazard a guess of the rate of vibration. Since energy is all a spirit is, it goes without saying that even a low crappy spirit is a higher vibration than I am capable of, BUT, I do see things sometimes, and so do others. When I taught classes, I always likened it to someone standing in the water with their head just below water level. You could stand up on your tippy toes and look above water level, but just for a few moments, then you had to come down.

I think it's the same thing with our vibration. You can raise it for a few moments, but then that Mexican food you had rumbles in your belly, or you think of someone that pissed you off. Think of all the material things that you need as a human. Money, food, warmth; a spirit needs none of these, they are detached from it, so naturally they are at a higher vibration than us. I always thought that was the truth, because I seldom saw a spirit for more than a few seconds. And I know that sometimes they really want to be seen, they seem to go out of their way to get my attention. I don't know how many times I had been doing readings for people and saw a wisp behind them, or around the room, over and over again. Like it was trying to get my attention, but I just was inches away from being able to, I couldn't. It's all good I guess.

Here was something that we should've been able to see, but didn't or couldn't. We could feel them, and hear them, but we couldn't see anything. Since what we felt over there was crappy, I don't think it wanted to be seen. That gets me off on another tangent.

I mentioned about my being able to see spirits at the beginning of the book, and like everything, it had continued to develop. Again, it wasn't seeing people, it was seeing wispy piles of smoke or a shimmer, like heat waves, but going downward, always downward. Sometimes there were little flashes of sparkles in them. Sometimes I saw balls of light. Sometimes I saw a shimmer with what looked like black beads in them.Sometimes, sometimes, sometimes. What the hell? Seriously, it was never the same, and I could never explain clearly what I'd seen, only particular instances. When people asked me,"What do they look like?" I was always hard-pressed to answer. I would get some disbelieving looks because it wasn't like what they had thought it would be. Sometimes I would see things that were solid black or dark grey, and they didn't like to be seen, they always moved.

Once I was investigating a house and I walked into a room where the client had been hearing things in the night. As we walked in, I saw a black shadow move behind her. So I took two steps and looked at her back, (changing my viewpoint), and it moved behind her again. I asked her to leave the room, and as she did, whatever it was, followed her and the room got brighter. It got brighter to the point that she noticed as well.

By the way, how do you tell people about stuff like that without freaking them out? Gently and couching it in good terms. So anyway, here I am, I can see pretty well, not every second of the day, but usually when I focus, and wondering how come I couldn't see anything that was rustling the leaves around us in Cogger's. It might be because it was low, and therefore black and hard to see in the dark and in the woods, or like I said, it didn't want to be seen.Either way, nada.Now down at the bottom of the hill, phew, that was a different story. I would sit there and talk and see 40 or 50 things, sometimes people standing there, sometimes wisps of smoke, sometimes pure clear grey or white.Again, sometimes, sometimes, sometimes.I also began to notice that going through the same EVP files again, I had missed a lot of the finer ones. I believe it was because after listening so often, my ears had become attuned to them. It was much like the people who study aerial reconnaissance photos. If you or I looked at them, we could barely make out a house, well, do it every day for a year or so and you can count bunkers. Re-listening to them, I found so many I had missed. My favorite was when I heard Chris say, "It's like we're surrounded by them, but they're weaker," and a spirit replied, "They're purer."**PLAY THEY'RE PURER EVP**That blew my mind. It sounded so clear that I didn't notice it the first time listening on CD in the truck. That EVP told me how, as spirits worked off their crap, they would be less and less able to interact with this world and hence become, "PURER". And that reaffirmed for me, (as someone who grew up and lived in haunted houses almost all his life), that when we hear of a haunted house, it's the usual case of a houseful of spirits, but there is one so dense, it's able to make itself known to us otherwise oblivious humans. My parents' house was a perfect example. Built by a miserable old relative with one arm, he was there, along with a ton of others, but he was the one dense enough to make himself known to our family. Now that I could see spirits, I hadn't been to one place, to one house, where they didn't show themselves to me. At first it freaked me out, think about it, ghosts are everywhere. There were no real haunted houses, this is a haunted world.

Let that sink in for a moment, will you.

Understand that regardless of your belief systems, science teaches us that energy never ends. What are we? We live in a haunted world, back to our story. When I first began to see spirits, I would react when I noticed something. People would look over their shoulders to see what I was staring at behind them. As time passed and I saw more and more, I grew accustomed to it and I came to realize that spirits were everywhere, some denser, some PURER, but everywhere, and constantly interacting with us.

Let me recap since this is an important thing that no one ever wants to think about. We live in a haunted world. There are spirits everywhere. Some are good, and they inspire us, others less so, and they try to make us do crappy things. If you read this and think, "Come on, when I was masturbating the other day, there were spirits in the room?"

Yes.

I would say that the good ones probably left you to your business, and the crappy ones watched, maybe feeding from that sexual energy. They have always been there, always will be.

"Are you telling me when I take a crap, there is something there beside me?"

Yes, that is exactly what I am saying. I don't know why or how, but I have seen many spirits in bathrooms. Don't ask me, I don't know why, and seriously, I really don't want to know if I wish to know why.

Think that energy never ends. It transforms. Accept that there is a world alongside of us. Maybe it is the 4th dimension, maybe the 72nd, I don't know, all I know is what I see.

When I was with the Shamans, I had been introduced to a woman named Michelle. She is a talented web designer and she was going to design the group's website. In exchange, we were going to teach her what we knew. As we talked about it amongst ourselves, all of a sudden I specifically volunteered to give her the Reiki attunements, part of me knew the others would wave hands like she was magically delicious and say, "You're a Reiki master now, voila." The other part of me wanted to get some practice giving attunements. I think that mostly, I was just following my intuition. So we met one fine day and I taught her Reiki. She and I quickly became friends, talking often on the phone and making each other laugh, she has a great sense of humor and a wonderful giggle. Now, Michelle was someone who didn't really believe in ghosts, I mean, some of us can entertain the idea mentally, but no one wants to think they are around us. So naturally I saw a challenge and had to take her down to Coggers with Chris and I. By this time a very clear, "NO TRESPASSING," sign had been posted at the Training School. I could only imagine what would transpire if we did walk down.

"What are you three people doing here on private property?" asked officer pain in the ass.

"Just getting attuned to energy sir," would be my reply.

"Get into the car son," he would say as he un-holstered his pistol.

Not happening. So we passed on that and headed straight down into the woods. Michelle is an easy laugh as we sat there next to the pond, talking and joking. To make sure we got some EVPs, I started talking of supernatural things. We recorded the best EVP ever ,(to me anyways). I was telling a story and very clearly among us you hear, "Hey," and a bunch of quick whistles. **PLAY HEY AND WHISTLES EVP**

At the end, while shehad felt a lot of things,(cold spots, tapping, and energy), she wasn't entirely convinced. We got some great EVP's and it wasn't until I played them for Michelle that her attitude about spirits started to change. You see, it's all well and fine to watch shows about it, talk about it, and even feel one or two things, but when you sit there for a couple hours in the dark and listen to recordings of voices that you KNOW you didn't hear, well, that tends to change things a bit. This is what happened with her.

Listening to the files, it was an amazing night for a few reasons. Besides a couple of the clear EVPs, we also recorded a quick three second drib of another language, that sounded Dutch or old Scottish.**PLAY ANOTHER LANGUAGE EVP** No matter who I played it for, no one knew or had any idea what it was. After we were done running energy and standing theresmudging at the top of the hill, we got three EVPs in seven seconds. Now, they are hard to make out, but you can clearly hear, "**shit, fuck it and burning**," as I am being smudged. **PLAY BURNING EVP** The fact of Michelle laughing like a hyena because she almost set my head on fire with glowing sage coals, makes it hard to get past. "Don't."Here was proof that being smudged did work. Here was what sounded like spirits complaining while I was being smudged. Seriously, how amazing is that? As I've always said to anyone who I taught, smudge works to a certain level of spirit, anything hardcore and you're just pissing it off. Here was clear proof from spirits that they didn't like it.

So Chris and I spent our second year investigating down Coggers, visiting every few weeks; to feel, to sense, and to learn. We were always asking questions, always putting theories about the place out there, and never getting any real answers, just more EVPs. Once or twice we heard that, "Reah," or whatever it was, the Coggers creature off in the distance. Always we would laugh, joke, sense, and feel and at the end of the night, we would run energy, sometimes ending up feeling great, sometimes coming out of there feeling heavy. Down in the woods I would always sit there and talk to him and ask "why?" "Why me, why here? Why did I grow up in this place? Why Coggers? He would always reply, "that's what I like about your Norm, you're after answers and you're not stopping till you get them"

"Why?"

One night as we came back to my house and I was smudging him, Chris said, "Holy shit, I just felt something run from the smudge across my head! It literally ran from it!"

"That's a stage five clinger I said," borrowing a line from Wedding Crashers.

"What the ell is a stage five clinger?" Chris' accent got worse when he was excited.

"It's a spirit that's the next level up from being affected by smudge, dense enough that you can feel, but too heavy to move with it," I said calmly, as I motioned for him to turn around and let me smudge his back.

"I just felt the fooking thing run to the front of my head." I could see an excited and scared glint in his eyes. "How do you get rid of it?"

"Keep yourself happy."

"What? Keep myself happy?"

"Yes, don't let it affect you, know that it's there, and keep yourself in the high vibe."

I had an idea how to get rid of it. It had taken me something like four months to figure out the one that I had gotten from Susan. I decided that it was time that Chris went through what I did as well. He looked at me a little wild eyed as I smugly smiled and reminded him of the simplest of lessons that the spirit world teaches us, "Keep yourself happy dude, that's the only way to get rid of it, don't let it feed off of you, don't let it affect you, stay in the good zone."

Easy for me to say, yes, I know, I wasn't the one going home with it.

It wasn't long after that, that Chris called me and said,"I think I am going to give the woods a break for a bit." He hemmed and hawed but eventually I asked him point blank,"Chris, it's because you are going to bed at 2:00 a.m., seeing someone standing at you bedside, staring at you?" He admitted it was, and I pointed out to him, "The thing is bud, they have always been there, always will be there, it's only through all the work you've done, that you've become aware of them."

That didn't change his mind too much, dammit, so we both took a break from the woods.

Some time afterwards I was teaching a Reiki level 1 class one summer night. I had four students. As I knelt in front of them, to give the attunement to someone, I heard very clearly a, "Rugglebebleah" of a spirit, it actually sounded like a raven, but in the room with us. I looked around at my other students, and no one seemed to have had heard anything. So I moved to the next student and continued on with the attunement process. I couldn't see anything in the room no matter how hard I tried and I had just heard that noise near that one person. Now usually in class after receiving a Reiki attunement, you practice giving Reiki to others, just to get you accustomed to feeling the energy. Well, as the students and I were practicing on the person whom I had heard the noise, one of them looked at me, and said, "Wow, that's so cool."

"What is?" I asked.

"I felt something run up my arms, and I got all light headed," she told me.

As I looked at her, I could see these dark circles appearing under her eyes. "Holy fuckhouse," I thought to myself. (Yes, I do say that, even being who I am). The attunement knocked something out of the first person's energy field into hers!!! I can't really talk about the spirit world during a Reiki 1 class. Reiki 1 is all about love and light, good feelings, happiness and peace. To talk about dark spirits and entities and attachments would just freak these women out, and probably get me arrested in some parts of the US.

"Ok cool, why don't you get on the table and let us run energy on you?" I told her and started to crank her heart open as she lay there. I spent a great deal of time on it. Eventually, after thinking, "Come to me, come to me, come to me," I felt something slimy and crappy crawl up my arms and ugh, it took me a few days to get rid of that!

Even though I was taking a break, always, when I would visit mom and dad's house, I would look toward Cogs and think about it. I felt it calling me and I dreamt about it often, but I stayed away. My kids would ask, "Dad, how come you don't take us fishing there anymore?" and I would use misdirection, "Hey kids, look a deer!" to change the subject. I didn't want to expose them to the spirits there, and certainly didn't want them to pick anything up. Even though their innocence was a form of protection for them, I was innocent like dirt, and didn't want them to get anything because of me.

As I took stock in my life during this time, I had a lot of things to be thankful for. Even though I had broken with my teachers and friends, I was doing readings at a prestigious metaphysical shop and doing fairly well teaching classes. I still didn't like my job, but I saw that I was the ultimate determiner of my attitude there. I began to be more open with everyone about the things I was doing and learning. No more was spirituality a dirty little secret. I began to ask co-workers in Spanish if they believed in ghosts and the spirit world. One day one of them mentioned he didn't believe in that stuff and would sleep in any haunted house he heard of. So, I invited him down Coggers with me. We sat down there and talked. I felt and saw, and he didn't. The following day when I played the EVPs for him, he said, "I don't hear anything," and looked uncomfortable and walked quickly away.

I guess for some of us, black and white is more comfortable then grey.

In the summer of 2009 I was working a psychic party for a friend at her house. Since she was a very spiritual woman, I wasn't surprised to be seeing lots of spirits in her office where I was doing the readings. Now, I must admit this fully, it had been the second day I was wearing my daily use contacts, and I had worked all day doing concrete, so I was very tired. As I sat there and read her friends, I was seeing more than the usual, and later in the evening while I held someone's palm and told them about their fate line, I blinked and I saw perfect.

I saw the spirit world perfectly.

All the spirits that were in the room, I could see. Like a filter had been placed over my eyes, and I could see the world as it truly was. I don't know how long my head darted here and there, but there was a long blue tubular thing with a white point of light, in motion, on my left, and a large red pillar of smoke behind that and something orange on my right. I couldn't believe it. I rubbed my eyes and looked again and it had shifted to energy, and I could see energy better than I ever have. I could make out the shapes, the outlines and details of everything that was around us. There was a ball of energy on my lap about two feet across and another here and another there. I looked everywhere about the room, and eventually the poor woman I was sitting with said to me,"Err, you were saying something about my life line?""Sorry," I replied and then I continued doing my reading for her. Later, when she was done and I waited for my next client, I couldn't see anything. I was shocked into silence and amazed. As I drove home that night, it was so poignant; I couldn't help thinking about what I had seen. Initially I thought to myself, "Hell no, I don't want to see that all the time, who could live like that?There's no way anyone could exist, seeing that all the time, no way, how could you even walk around?" I wouldn't want to walk through a giant ball of energy I knew was a spirit. Another part of me realized what a gift it had been. I started wanting to see that way again, so I tried to see even more. Every time it crossed my mind I would tilt my head and peek around. Looking here and there, hoping it would kick in like it had that night. It never did to the same degree, but everywhere I was, I would see them. Everywhere.

When I talk to people about the spirit world, it bothers them. I know it does. I see their face change when I mention this. No one wants to think that everywhere is haunted, that we live in a haunted world.

We do. We all live haunted lives, we just don't know about it.

We want the comfort of only reading or hearing about ghosts safely from our own home. Few are comfortable with the idea that something is laying there watching them. That as you read this, there are spirits with you.

They are

Back to our story.

I didn't go to Cogs much during the summer of that year. A few times I took friends, to show and teach them about the spirit world. One of them couldn't believe the files I had sent him were EVPs, since they were so clear in comparison to what he heard when he watched Ghost shows on TV. So we went to Coggers and spent a few hours sitting there, chatting like magpies and eventually I brought the conversation around to the afterlife. While talking about the spirit world and life and everything in the universe, he said, "I don't know if there's a God, or if we are just drifting through space here." Right after he said, "I don't know if there's a God," we got a clear, "YES."**PLAY YES EVP**

Think about that for a moment, will you? Who do you think would know better, an atheist or a ghost?

A couple of times I went with Chris, and once a friend of his visited from England, so we took him and got some crisp EVPs. How cool is it to be there with two men, and hear very clearly, "hmmmm," in a female voice?**PLAY HMMMM EVP** We also got an answer when we were down there when we asked for the thousandth time, "Why are you here." (I would always ask this, and say "why here?" I would want to spend the afterlife in the women's locker room at ULOWELL)."Healing," was the reply we recorded. **PLAY HEALING EVP**

That blew me away! Healing? Whaaaaatttt?Coggers and healing? I hadn't even thought of it that way, not one time. That something could be down there trying to heal or was going to be healed. Sometimes when we were sitting there, we would feel that dense crappy energy of whatever had screamed at us, and we would have to work on opening our hearts even more, to try and keep it away.I do believe that those open hearts were keeping it away. Sometimes it just plain hurt to sit there. Now they are saying they are down there for healing????That doesn't make sense to me. Once we were sitting there and it was feeling particularly creepy and I said, "Lets run some Reiki!" having by this time, made him a Reiki master as well. The following day when listening to the EVPs I heard, "You're sexy". **PLAY YOU'RE SEXY EVP** We also got somewhat threatened by the spirit world when it told us, "We can find you."**PLAY FIND YOU EVP**

That's great, now they are telling us that we will get visited. I knew Cogger's was haunted, I didn't think it was haunted by the mob.

When I started researching this, and writing this book, I went down one late winter night with Chris. My research had yielded some names of old Training School headmasters, and some names of people who had died down Coggers. I wanted to use them and see if I got any responses. We had had a couple of warm February days and not being from New England, Chris walked down the hill and walked right up and placed all his weight on the ice and went right through, soaking his foot. Tears of laughter ran down my cheeks as he stood there and shook off his foot and complained about being wet. I told him,"I can tell you didn't grow up in New England, you don't touch the edge of pond ice after a couple of warm day's man."

"I thought it would be safe," he replied.

"Look, all your spirituality is thrown right out the window with a wet foot." I stood there giggling uncontrollably.

"Idiot,"we got on **EVP. PLAY IDIOT EVP**

As spiritual as I want to be, or am, I had great delight in emailing him that file, laughing about it again.

A few months later, we were back down there, and talking with a friend we had brought. I mentioned the "healing EVP" and asked if that's why they were here. And I got a clear response,"Yes", and it really threw me for a loop. **PLAY YES TO HEALING EVP** It truly made me look at Coggers in a different light. I battled with it for a long time. Healing? Wtf? Why healing? Did healing have to do with what was there? Why there? What the hell were they doing there? Were Chris and I in some way healing them? Was the place itself healing for them? And what the hell was the Coggers creature about anyway? We also recorded, "Let the power build up," when we were running energy. **PLAY LET THE POWER BUILD UP EVP** As in, one spirit speaking with another, saying, "Let the power build up," before you walk in and take some.

CHAPTER 16

That's it. That's my story. That's the one I'm telling and I'm sticking to it, well, the one about the woods anyway.

I went from remembering Coggers with love and fear, to a deeper understanding of life and what it holds for all of us in the end. I changed from being a selfish miserable person, to being someone who wishes to do kindness every chance I can. From thinking that Coggers was haunted by evil spirits, whose sole purpose was to scare the shit out of me and if IT was lucky, one day eat my brains, to understanding that the spirit world is much like life, there are good people, and bad, wherever you might be. I believe that most of the spirits down there weren't there to kill my friends and I, but down there for a purpose that I cannot comprehend. Why Coggers? Why that place? Was it because of the reform school? Did the spirits drift from the Training School to Coggers? Did they perceive something my eyes cannot, and as such, were drawn to the pond and the woods? Was the Coggers creature from the reform school or was the reform school a symptom of the Coggers creature? So which came first, the chicken or the egg? I know the reform school is haunted. I know it, with every fiber of my being I do. Too many bad things happened there, too many tears, too many sad kids for that energy not to be imprinted there. Also, we have the "School" EVPcollected on one of the first times there, when I asked, "Why are you here?"**PLAY SCHOOL EVP** This was such a nice confirmation for me. I wish I could've gotten permission to collect EVPs at the Training School, but it ain't happening. Personally, as I've always said, I think something was always in Coggers. I think whatever is there, is older than anything we can imagine. I think it was old when the Native Americans avoided the place because it feels that way to me. It's too strong to be a spirit or a shade. If your average poltergeist is a karate practitioner, this thing there was Bruce Lee. I won't go into the numerous dreams I've had of Coggers, so many, so damn many, most of them showing me something that isn't what we would term normal ,(not that any of this is normal Ha-ha).

    Whenever I talked to people down there, or about it, I would always mention the fact that EVPs take a tremendous amount of energy for a spirit. That's why most of them are only one or two words, and never more than five. Now, I would say energy workers will get better EVPs than the average person because their energy fields are stronger, hence the spirit is more able to utilize it. But even so, the longest EVP we ever got was, "May he rise up," or "Get down here." But they are of a much clearer quality than the average person gets. The Coggers creature, well, it would break its ass through into our world to the point where my friends and I,(as unaware, disbelieving kids), could hear it, get the shit scared out of ourselves and run for our lives. It could make itself visible, or not, move trees and branches, sound like poor imitations of animals, and basically do everything a spirit could, but with a hell of a lot more power. That doesn't sound like any ghost I've ever heard of. I am not going to say its evil, but I think a lot of its intentions were malicious. It never came across as a glowing white shade, with messages from loved ones. It came out as some screaming, barking thing, as a dog chasing me through the woods, as something that enjoyed scaring people. Again, I think that the energy was there before the school, and that it enjoyed the negative emotion. It fed from it, and damn right it suggested all sorts of nasty things in the unknowing ears of kids playing or the guards working there over the years.

While researching the area, I came across numerous references to King Philip's War and how the Wamesit Indians were slaughtered in Chelmsford. Now naturally, I would love to claim it was there, in Coggers, that they were killed. But I cannot with good conscience. It would be too easy, it would be a copout to say that. All the different EVPs I got, "onahehe," and "boopah," **PLAY BOOPAHULAH EVP** would tend to lend some credence to this, but since it happened over 300 years ago, we will never know the location of where they died. People back then tended to say, "Yeah those Indians died good," and forget about it. I do know of numerous deaths down there, people drowning in the pond, workers dying in the sand and gravel company. And that is the legitimate proof that I got from the old newspapers via microfilm. Pulling those out of newspaper archives was more painful than passing a kidney stone, (I hope).

There are even more rumors that I encountered when talking to the people who lived there. They consist of happy, light hearted tales such as buses falling into the pond, kids drowning, Chilean soccer teams crashing on top of Brownie Hill and eating each other before venturing to leave. Personally, I know of two deaths. One, Larry Cox, a young man who went to swim across the pond one night when he was half drunk, while still in his clothes, and the other was a homeless man who lived down there for a couple of years.

When the gravel company was active, they had a giant steel cylinder that they would roll gravel through. The gravel was put in on one side and it would tumble out the other end, smaller and more rounded. Somehow this thing got discarded in the middle of the woods when they dismantled the place. This man lived in this cylinder for a couple of years. Truly and honestly, he lived out in the woods, went slowly insane and then rumor had it he was found dead in the giant rusty cylinder. What do I mean about him going insane? Well, about the time Katrina and I got freaked out, my friends and I harassed him as we searched the woods that night. He was normal and able to hold conversations then, and two years later, I was walking out of the woods, he came across me.

"Hey," I said.

"Hi, I've been thinking about working on this place and covering it," he replied.

"What, the woods?" I asked, looking around for what he was talking about.

"Yeah, it would help keep it warmer in the winter," he smiled sagely.

"Ha-ha yeah it would at that, but it might take a little work." Even in my semi stupor I knew this wasn't a good sign.

"Can I count on you to give me a hand when I start?" he asked.

"Oh yeah man, you see me all the time, just let me know." I could always just cut around the woods for awhileso I had to get along with him.

"It's gonna take a lot of wood, but I think I can find it around here,"he smiled and waved his hand behind him.

"You're gonna cut down the trees?"I asked.

"No, just collect it up, from the laying around, it's everywhere here."

I was thinking that if you cut down every tree there, and then all the trees in the neighborhood around, you would still run short of wood. He looked at me intently all of a sudden.

"You know where I remember you from? From the 60's man, you were a Yankees fan, but back then, DiMaggio he had no say," he said with a straight face and all sincerity.

WTF???

"Oh yeah dude, I loved the Yankees back then, hey ummm, I gotta get running, you know, can't let the girlfriend get mad at me by being late." Being close to his latent insanity was beginning to make me decidedly uncomfortable.

So did the woods make him crazy or was he crazy and the woods brought it out. I don't know, and kind of have my own assumptions. You can guess what they are.

I ran into him a few more times over the year. Once it was kind of scary, because for whatever reason, he was angry and was raking the dirt as my girlfriend and I walked past him. He freaked her out that day. Nothing like watching someone rake sand in anger to make someone wonder about the definition of insanity. The following year, running into an old friend from the neighborhood, he told me, "Hey you know that homeless guy living in the tube out in Coggers? He died."Being only 20 or so I really didn't care, other than that part of my mind that registered, "Huh, someone else died in Coggers." Again, there was something else, something besides the run of the mill human spirit, something else a bit darker than, "Bobbi."I guess we will never know or at least until this sells millions of copies then I can devote my whole life to finding out, and spend days and days on end down there. Then spend thousands of dollars being healed afterward, because lord knows the mental cost of hanging out there night after night. You might look at me and say, "Norman, after three years and dozens of investigations, you still don't know what is up with that place?" To which my answer is, "Shut up."

Ha-ha. You don't understand. Even being gifted, it's so overwhelming, so hard to tap into one spirit to feel his drama when four other spirits are bouncing off your skull.

When I first started teaching Chris down there, I thought that most spirits we interacted with were lost, mindless souls, hanging onto judgments, hanging onto their misguided perception of right and wrong and keeping themselves from entering heaven and knowing peace. I knew there were spirits that fed from our energy and dysfunctions, those that wanted to scare us and make us feel crappy. I believed that through holding love in my heart, I could show and remind them of it and heal them. Cross them if you will. I assumed for some reason, Coggers was a collecting point for them. In the beginning of my path, I thought some houses were haunted, and some places. Now I realize, ever since seeing clearly at that party, that **everywhere** is haunted and the spirit world is always interacting with us, always around us, good and bad. NO ONE likes to think that, "why just yesterday I was picking my nose," or "I was masturbating!" YES, YOUR GUIDES AND OTHER SPIRITS WERE THERE WATCHING YOU. It's always been that way, it always will be that way. We are not humans on a spiritual journey, we are spirits on a human journey.

Now I know it's different. That most of them are just working off crap they suffered in life until they understand that the material world doesn't matter. Until they learn that this life, while wonderful, is a pale shade of everything that lies beyond. But again I ask, why Coggers? Why that place? What makes it special? What makes it so easy for things to communicate through? After dozens of investigations, countless times recording, endless theories and lots of cups of Starbucks down there, I think it's the place itself. I think it's what we call "a thin spot" that is, a place where the boundary between worlds is thin, and for some reason, it's just that much closer to the other side than everywhere else. During my time of learning, I heard of the "veil" so many times, and it was assumed that I knew what it was. Well, I didn't, but I learned the VEIL is the fabric that separates this dimension from the next. I think for some reason, the veil in Coggers is thin, as it is in some houses. That spirits can come through a lot more clearly, and with a lot more force in thin spots. There are places called, "Ley Lines" which are supposed lines of force or psychic power that run around the planet. For skeptics, please go on the American Medical Association's website and look up all the support they have for the benefits of acupuncture. Now, think of a Ley line as the earth's Chi. When two of these lines cross, they form a "Ley Point" and it is thought that Stonehenge is a Ley Point or Macchu Picchu is a Ley Point, etc,etc. Many times down there, I theorized that Coggers might have been a Ley Point, but I never got a response. Even though I have no proof, I think that whatever is there, is trapped in that great triangle of woods, and will remain so, until it works through its issues.

Given the way it acts and what it likes doing, maybe a couple thousand years or so.

In the spring of 2010, I started getting blown away by the EVPs because they were telling us,"healing." I cannot tell you how that shook what I thought of the woods and its environs. Because maybe for some reason they were there for some kind of healing that I couldn't perceive, or maybe they were gathering waiting for us to run energy as we heard in, "Let the power build up."**PLAY LET THE POWER BUILD UP EVP** Either way, all of them weren't there to cause evil and horror like I had thought at some point. So many times, Chris had doubted the good we were doing there. I would and could point out the change in EVPs and the qualities of them, (from Reh and Die to Hi and hello), and how we seemed to collect less and less malicious ones the more we visited. Even sitting at the bottom of the hill wasn't bad anymore, and one night while down there with a friend, Chris commented, "Sometimes it was so hard to come down here,"and the spirit world replied,"Don't come down here."**PLAY DON'T COME DOWN HERE EVP**

It was a good New England ghosts way of saying, "Stop your bitching,"even for a ghost.

Cogger's remains the most haunted place I've even read about, let alone heard of. But I was no longer afraid of it. It would be easy for me to sit here and say, "I was never afraid again," or that "I learned everything, and blah blahblah," and make up a bunch of mystical shit. I won't lie; I won't do that to myself, or to you. There were times that I sat there, and had to try so hard to get rid of the fear that I felt.

But I succeeded.

I know that we did good down there, it feels different. At first, at the bottom of the hill, while looking at a pretty pond at night, you would feel unsettled and disquieted. Now, you can sit down there all night long and not sense a thing, or at least not be freaked out as much. I know that all the energy we ran helped in some way. Hell, let the power build up is a perfect example of how, like junkies, the spirit world was digging whatever we were doing. One night after Chris and I were there, I was listening to the EVPs and I heard so clearly, a woman's voice,"Thank you, thank you."**PLAY THANK YOU EVP** I know that it was meant for us, that somehow in some way, we had helped her. I like to think it was the woman whom I sensed that Halloween night, so long ago. That in some manner, in some way, we had done something for her, it was a nice feeling for a change. Down the path was different. A hundred times of running energy down there wasn't going to change it. The spirit there was too angry, to frustrated to listen to me. It delighted in making people afraid, as Andy said.

I started taking my kids fishing down there again, the first time in a long time, in the summer of 2010. I was so excited to see that the long summer sunny days had dropped the water level to where I remembered it as a child. So that for the first time in many years, the pond resembled, even slightly, the Coggers I had fished in my youth. I don't think they understood my glee as I pulled the boat ashore and walked around saying,"Look at this, when I was a kid, we used to___ here," over and over. It had been so many years since I had walked on some of the places, it reminded me of all the great times I had had there with Eric and my other friends. At the end of the day when I pulled the boat up the hill, I had to send my son to get my daughter at my parents' house, to help us carry the boat back.

As I stood up there and looked out, I could feel the presence of whatever it was that had haunted me as a child, that heaviness that sometimes was there, that thing that came out that night, screaming at us.

"Hey dude, love this place," I said out loud, and because I am a man, and a concrete worker at heart, finding I had to pee, I looked around and unzipped and started peeing. "Reahaha," I heard right next to me a moment later. It made me jump and zip up, thinking my kids had come up without me hearing them. I turned and found no one, and I chuckled, and said,"You got me good then you prick," but I had to laugh.

It was a good joke and I am sure for it, it was worth the energy it expended. But I had to smile, I was no longer afraid of it or really anything. I would never be afraid again for any period of time, ever. Shove a gun in my nose and tell me you're going to shoot me and I'm going to smile, and decide, this is the time that God is calling me home. **I trust**. As I stood up there and looked out, I realized it was and is still, (even with most of it gone), a wonderful place to grow up. As an adult, it's a wonderful place to go and teach about the spirit world, and to try and help those on the other side while doing so. Also great to stop and smell the swampy earthy smell, and think of times long past and laughter long gone.

A few weeks later, I went down Coggers by myself to prove that I had overcome my fear. I knew there was a chance that the dark heavy spirit could come out, and I would have to fight it with my love. Ha-ha, doesn't that sound like a joke, "fight it with my love," but I knew that with my open heart and hence, lack of fear, would be the only thing to protect me. As I sat down there and activated my recorders, I looked about the pond and was amazed at how nice it looked. How nice it felt to be there, and how I loved that place. I alternately felt afraid and happy, good and bad. Waves of emotion washed over me as I contemplated myself, and remembered. As per usual, there were all sorts of taps and noises. I watched the beaver cruise silently around, and all of a sudden my heart hurt. As I focused on opening it, and remembering good things, I felt afraid. It took a few minutes to get rid of it, but I felt it, and I had to smile. For the first time, I spoke out loud and honored the spirits. Apologizing to them for not being more respectful while I was down there, saying how I needed their help, in so many ways in my life, but more importantly in learning about the afterlife as they knew it. As I felt someone crawling up my legs, I blew some sage at them. (Not cool, I want to learn, but not have you dry humping me for six months.).All in all, it was a perfect night. I felt and experienced as I normally do, and since I am my own best friend, I made myself laugh and enjoyed my time there. I had mom meet me at the top of the hill to smudge me, since I didn't want to take anyone home. As I waited, I had to call her, and she told me, "I'm not going into those woods by myself." So I had to guide her in the 20 feet or so, but I understood what she meant. They do give off spookiness at night. It made me remember the first time my friend Andy bragged to me, "Dude we walked through Coggers BY OURSELVES tonight." I had to laugh, and as such, elicited a strange look from mom.

CHAPTER 17

I told you I lived a haunted life. That's just a small part of my experiences, (an important one to be sure). In my years, I think I have seen every single thing the spirit world can do. My whole life I've been fascinated with the supernatural, virtually every subject or aspect of it. I studied or read about it at some point. If you knew me in my 20's and we spent time together, chances are we would have talked about Cogger's or ghosts, etc., etc. I would have brought it up.I had a vast library of ghost related books that I would read, but then stop when I started creeping myself out and noticing taps more than usual. If we sit there in the daytime and speak about things that have happened, well chances are, you're not going home to a haunted house. Usually I was. I would go home and think of conversations or read my ghost books and then hear tapping, always tapping. Always they were trying to get my attention. Often, I was scared.

At some point in my life I bought a copy of Colin Wilson's excellent book, "The Encyclopedia of the

Unknown."As is my wont, since it is a good book, I re-read it occasionally. After I was healed, (it really is a great book), in a chapter labeled, "Possession," I found a reference to an author called, "Kardec."What Kardec explained was possession, and indeed his views on the spirit world rang true to me. I remember calling one of the Shaman's with it and reading it to her, to which she replied, "Why that sounds like what we believe."

Kardec wrote this about 150 years ago.

"According to *The Spirits Book* man consists of a body, "aura", intelligent soul and spiritual soul. The aim of human life, according to the spirits, is evolution, and this comes about through reincarnation- rebirth into new bodies. People who die suddenly, or are unprepared for death through reason of wasted lives, are often unaware that they are dead and become homeless, wanderers of the earth, attracted by human beings of like mind, and sharing their live and experiences. They are able, to some extent, to influence these like-minded people and make them do their will through suggestion. Some " low" spirits are activated by malice, others are merely mischievous and can use energy drawn from human beings to cause physical disturbances- these are known as poltergeists. When Kardec asked, "Do spirits influence our thoughts and actions?" the answer was, "their influence [upon human beings] is greater than you suppose, for it very often they who direct both." Asked about possession, the "spirit" explained that a spirit cannot actually take over another person's body, since that belong to the owner; but a spirit can assimilate itself into a person who has the same defects and qualities as himself and may dominate a such a person"
"The Mammoth Book of the Unsolved" Colin Wilson Pg 417

This is pretty much spot on what the Shamans were teaching. A few years later I came across his book, "A Guide to Mediumship," at a place where I was working. Seeing the name,

I bought it and it sat in my bag for a few months. Every time I went to read it, I was stopped cold by its sheer boredom. (I love to read and can force myself to toil through any book, well this, this was bad.) I think it had to do with 50 pages of him trying to convince the reader that the spirit world was real. Remember, he wrote it in the 1850's. When I did skip ahead, I found he,(Kardec), was asking questions of a medium, (remember the Shamans channeling Jesus and such), well, Kardec would ask a series of questions and receive answers. This particular book was all about mediumship, the different kinds of mediums, how to develop skills and things to be aware of. If you ever have an interest in such a practice, I would recommend starting here. See, the thing is, as I read, I Googled Kardec and started reading his biography. Here's what Wikipedia showed me: "**Allan Kardec** is the pen name of the French teacher and educator **Hippolyte Léon DenizardRivail** (Lyon, October 3, 1804 – Paris, March 31, 1869). He is known today as the systematizer of Spiritism for which he laid the foundation with the five books of the Spiritist Codification."

Basically, if you go to a Spiritualist Church, their teachings are based off of Kardec. If you go to a medium, they are trained in Kardecs teachings and manners. To me, this was the real deal. Here was information from the horse's mouth, and given who I am, this is what I wanted. The quote I had read in the "Encyclopedia of Unsolved Mysteries" came from a book called, "The Spirits Guide." It was 1001 questions asked in a systematic order, an attempt if you will to gain knowledge and insight into pretty much everything. If you ever want to learn about the spirit world, please, do yourself a favor, don't take a class, just read this book. Kardec was the first to sit down with a medium and a list of questions to systematically try to learn all he could about whatever they could teach. Seriously, don't listen to anyone who claims to know the answers, just read The Spirits Book.

It was reading this book that everything, and I mean EVERYTHING I had seen and experienced made sense. Everything. This book answered all those, "why's" that I had asked Chris. Why I grew up there, why Coggers was haunted, why spirits fed from energy, why some of them hung around people.

Why's, all the why's that no self proclaimed Shaman could ever answer for me.

Trust me on this, if you have experienced the supernatural, or believe in ghosts. READ THIS BOOK. Don't take another's word for it, chances are, they are screwing up the message. When I began to understand all the whys, well that ended my study of the spirit world. They,(the spirit world), had achieved their goal, to get me to my answer of the "why" so that it could unfold my next journey, my next phase of my life.

Don't get me wrong. I still go to haunted houses and visit Cog's occasionally, but I consider it a hobby. Once I understood the, "why" of it, I was so humbled. So much effort had been made on my behalf, I was and am indebted.

When I talk to people about the spirit world, inevitably I always say, "It's taught me to enjoy life, be kind, and have fun." It has taught me these things, and so much more. It's given me a greater perspective on life itself. The healing I went through, that I was blessed with, all of the cases of possession that I have seen, all have taught me what matters in life. What's important? Not much. Lol, the way we feel about the ones we love, the way we act towards each other, kindness and compassion, love, everything our society and world teaches us doesn't matter.

Everything we lose sight of in the quest for that brass ring that everyone wants. Jesus said, "It is easier for a camel to go through the eye of a needle, than for a rich man to enter the kingdom of Heaven." Why? Because, (and I am generalizing), people tend to lose their compassion as they become wealthier. Maybe that's the cost, or part of the process, but I know that it's hard for Donald Trump to understand what it's like to worry about making the electric bill payment. It's even harder for him to sympathize with someone worrying about it. I am not saying the rich don't suffer, of course they do, we all do. What I am saying is they have a harder time being compassionate to those less fortunate than they. This is what I think the scripture meant. I believe the highest my soul can evolve to, is a place of love and compassion. Understanding for others and a willingness to help in any way I can, without thinking of what I am going to get out of it. Compassion. What the hell is your Mercedes going to matter if you get stomach cancer? What does any material item mean when you compare it to love? While I cannot sit here and pay my bills with love or feed my kids with it, love will enable me to go through life hell of a lot easier then lack of it.

When you look at the course of your life, are you going to say, "I am so glad I was kind and helpful to almost everyone I met," or will you say, "Yes, I got that mansion and Hummer I always wanted?" I believe that is what the spirit world is learning on the other side, compassion and love. What better way to understand humanity and what motivates it then watching them for 300 years, (or however long it takes you to understand them). No, love is all that matters in this world, and it's with love that God created it, and from love that most of us are made. Neal Walsch says that everything boils down to love and fear. Every emotion at its base is one or the other. Greed? Fear of being poor? Anger? Fear of whatever is making you angry, (a copout, I know). I agree with this. Everything has shown me this to be true.

What's love and fear? Selfish and selflessness. I fear being poor so I act with greed. I fear someone's attitude towards me, so I get angry. And on the flip side, I love people, so I reach into my pocket and give some homeless person my last five dollars. Selfish and selfless.

  Everything good and light, comes from love, everything negative, from fear. I see a distinct lack of love everywhere I look. I don't think that's my cynical perception of the world, merely my observation. Can anyone tell me that society teaches selflessness? Can anyone tell me that they think our society teaches compassion? Since, "man falls in love and lives a good life," won't get you to watch the news at 11, the media feeds from fear. Breeds it and propagates it, and tries to shock you into watching them, to living in fear, and being afraid not to watch. As I write this, and I think of humanity as a whole, or the little part that I see and have seen, I have concerns, (I won't worry, never ever worry again). I will leave it to the gurus and the other professional psychics to tell what they see for the future of our species. I am concerned because to me, when I look about me, and watch the world, I see very little compassion. I see selfishness everywhere, and that doesn't bode well for us. People are in such a rush all the time, cutting each other off, driving, going, going, going, get out of my way, I was here first. Where are they going? Nowhere fast. Driving home,, getting in two minutes earlier than I would have if I took my time and let someone else go in front of me. What have I gained? Not much. In essence, I see so many others exactly as I used to be, and I know from personal experience, that isn't really a good thing. Every single moment of life is so wonderful. Every time we talk or interact with another person it is an opportunity to make their day better, their lives better, to spin out infinite ripples of potential good. So often we shove them aside, and think,"Get the fuck out of my way," instead of smiling and opening the door, instead of looking at them with compassion, for what are they, but like us. Drifting through life, feeling alone, feeling afraid and confused, and ultimately in fear.

That's what I've learned from spirits about life and the evolution of our souls, but they have taught me so much more than that. I realize now that we are constantly surrounded by spirits. Not even realize, but I know it. Every single moment of every single day, there are spirits interacting with us. Some of them are nasty and attach to our energy fields, feeding from our dysfunctions, others from our addictions. That voice that says, "steal that,""take this," and "leave them there," jeering, mocking us. Some have our highest intentions at heart and are there to support us and help us along our journey through life's path, to help our souls evolve. The crappy spirits, the ones we always hear about in books and TV shows, the ones that can make us otherwise oblivious people aware, they are the opposite of love. They feed from all the negativity of life. Most of them feed from fear. They love scaring people and get stronger when they do. Others love to suggest to tell you to take that drug or drink another beer, or, "smack him, you don't have to put up with that shit."Always, always, it returns to our greatest gift, choice. We choose how we will react, and what we will do.

When I see "Ghost Tours here!" or "investigate this haunted house," I always cringe, because people have no idea what they are taking home with them and even less, do they know how to get rid of it. When I tell friends and people I know about Coggers and the spirit world, they always say, "I want to go." I wouldn't do that to my worst enemy. Once I mention that stuff can come home with them, their attitude tends to change. Again, I feel bad when I see these tours, for a few different reasons. The people running the tour, they are trying to make money from the spirit world, they are not standing there, running light and love and compassion, trying to help them. They are taking people around saying, "Look at this, isn't this creepy!"Tend, they are usually sensitive's, who have experienced something of the spirit world, hence their interest. Well, since they are sensitive, they will attract stuff, and take it home and then wonder where those crazy thoughts come from.

DON'T GO ON GHOST TOURS, not unless you enjoy feeling like crap.

The good spirits, the evolved ones, the ones trying to help, they are always there as well. I tell people, "Think of it this way, if I died today, I would go and hang around my kids – yeah, to fuck with them once and a while, but more to offer them love and compassion when they are scared, and depressed, to be there for them." We all have spirits like that around us. The spiritual community calls them your "guides"as guiding spirits designed to help you along your life's journey. They can suggest, they can tell you things via the dream world, but ultimately, they are there to help. I have read so many ways online and in books to communicate with them, but I never ever heard a voice, or had someone appear. But you know what? There are a man and a woman, who are in 30% of my dreams, and they are always helping me. Those are guides. That good voice that says, "Take this, get an extra one, call this person," those are guides. Always listen to that voice, always look and be aware.

In February of 2011, I, and a select few, were chosen to go to Peru. There, we flew over the Andes and landed in Puerto Maldonado, in the Amazon. We stayed for two weeks at a center ran by a Shaman there. It was there that I did Ayahuasca. Let me say, Ayahuasca is real. What I had read, about the South American belief on Shamanism was real as well. Some people are better at it than others. I and about 10 others participated in the Ayahuasca ceremony, and as I lay in the jungle waiting for it to take effect, (we were all individually, in screened in rooms in the jungle), I heard a female crying off somewhere to my left and then a male voice screamed. Very, very clearly, a voice in my head told me, "Ayahuasca tailors itself to the individual, so that each gets what they need from it."

Then I went on my own journey, a thousand miles in one night, vision after vision. An endless series of teachings, with me asking questions and being shown what I wanted and didn't want to know. Some of them have come true since, others, I await. The next day we gathered around and spoke of what we saw. Some saw nothing, others had visions like I did. It was then that I realized that I was a Shaman, if I so chose to be. That I had a gift, that I could use for the benefits of others.

I choose not to be. I was shown by vision that my journey is different, that I had a choice, I chose another path. When I was there I saw amazing personal transformations in those I met in Peru, some of them startling, and well, I learned that plant medicine is real. I learned there that Shamanism is far different than what everyone in the US wants us to think. That it is ancient and powerful beyond our comprehension and not to be trifled with, but to be treated with the respect it deserves. I felt clean leaving the jungle, mentally crisp, as if all the junk I had accumulated over the years was washed away. When I came back home, I found my ability to see spirits had diminished. It wasn't completely gone, but I didn't see them as clearly or as often. I would guess it was because I was shown my next steps and they didn't involve the spirit world. Which also what reading Kardec had taught me, that there was a reason for my haunted life, once I discovered it, it was time to move to my souls next evolution. Reading Kardec just confirmed what I had seen. Our attitudes and beliefs affect what we attract to us. If I think everyone sucks and life sucks, then you can be damn sure there's spirits around me feeding into that energy, telling me that everyone sucks, why? Sometimes shitty people, (or spirits), take comfort when people are as weak as them. Or like my friends who believe in angels and hold them and life perfect, that's what they attract and they seem so ethereal at times to me. After attracting so much suckage in my life, for so many years, I think it would be nice to think of angels.Personally, I choose the latter. Ever since I heard the EVP (they're purer) I've contemplated what it means to be purer. What would it mean to a spirit? To a human?To all of us? I thought that as I worked, or as a spirit worked its shit off in the next life and worked off its anger issues, frustrations, wants and desires, it would become purer. As it saw that ultimately, we are all the same, all afraid, all alone, and drifting through life, it would evolve to a more compassionate place and hence, become purer. I thought about what that means to us. All those wants and things we think we want, they serve to frustrate us, all those things we think we need. Stress? This year CNN reported that 118 million antidepressants were prescribed by doctors. Now assuming that every person that takes them, is addicted,(yes, I know, but bear with my thought train,) and takes and gets 30 prescriptions a year, that's roughly 4 million people in the US on some kind of drug to make themselves feel better! TV, society tells us that shit we don't need will make us happy, so we get it, we brag about it, and get an energy fix from telling people about it and their attention to us. Once that wears off, "Dude, I don't want to hear about your plasma TV again," we feel empty, and we look for another thing to throw into it to fill the empty hole we feel inside. So we spend more and more, feeling worse and worse and then we see that commercial,"Hey, if sometimes you're not happy, you should take this pill."

    Bah.

"Do you feel unhappy? Do you worry? Do you breathe a lot? Well, we got a pill to make these things go away."

Bah.

I know that any spirit would give its left testicle to live again, and have another shot at life. I once wrote "would you trade the memories of a thousand lives, just to live once again?" Well, you have.

Everyone wants a lovely perfect life, yet few stop to think that everyone suffers, EVERYONE. Here is Norman Shaw's definition of stress, please feel free to correct me, but you won't. Stress is a person, place or thing that you are trying to control. That's it, something that you want to control, and since you can't, you're freaking yourself out. What can you truly control? One thing, and its virtually impossible - your own attitude. That's all you've been granted dominion over. Everything else is placed in your life's path by God, for you to choose to learn from or not. Let go of your illusion. You can't control anything, so stop trying, and stop stressing out. Accept, enjoy and be happy. Life is so damn good, every moment, every single day. Good and bad, happy and sad, everything is to be felt and lived. I see people say, "Life sucks," and I can't imagine how far I have come, that I have difficulty remembering I was once that way too. Life is so good, remember it, believe it, and make it so. Personally, I've come to learn something simple, yet profound.

Life is the ultimate gift. Each and every second of it, the whole range of emotions is a gift to you. Live it that way and you will never regret.

Society teaches us that we deserve more; we deserve an endless series of good days.

That isn't life.

Life is hard and easy, it's sad and inspiring, good and bad, life is life, and you must embrace every second of it, every emotion must be felt and enjoyed. As my favorite Persian poet Rumi says in Guest House:

> This being human is a guest house.
> Every morning a new arrival.
> A joy, a depression, a meanness,
> some momentary awareness comes
> as an unexpected visitor.
> Welcome and entertain them all!
> Even if they're a crowd of sorrows,
> who violently sweep your house
> empty of its furniture,
> still, treat each guest honorably.
>
> He may be clearing you out
> for some new delight.
> The dark thought, the shame, the malice,
> meet them at the door laughing,
> and invite them in.
> Be grateful for whoever comes,
> because each has been sent
> as a guide from beyond.

You know my thoughts about, "A guide from beyond."

Life, the ultimate gift, what is sin? Ruining someone else's gift, check out the commandments. What do they say? Don't covet your neighbor's house, wife. Don't lie, honor your parents. Don't steal. In essence, making someone else's day shitty. Thou shall not worship other gods, making God's day shitty. As I said, at the end of your days, will you celebrate living in a $600,000 house, or the time you helped someone and made their life better? You know what I think.

I always hear people talking about the meaning of life. "What's the reason we are here?" It's the age-old philosophical question isn't it? It is so simple, and it's what I've learned from the spirit world. You are here to evolve your soul and everything that occurs to you in your life, serves that purpose. The best part is, Purpose doesn't give a shit whether you like it or not, it just is. Ha ha, simple isn't it? Some would say too simple. I don't think so, because the best things in life are simple like that. I ask of you now, examine your life, and look at times that you felt stressed out, worried and at the end of your rope and then remember how it turned out. Therein lies the perfection of life, that all things are designed to teach. That's the meaning of life, to evolve your soul to a better place so that you are prepared for your next lesson.

Sometimes people ask me, "Would you do anything different? If you could do your life over, what would you change?" I always shock them, and say, "Nothing, I would do it exactly the same." It's usually startling to them because we will be working and sweating and slowly dying together on some rude jobsite somewhere. But it's true. Everything in my life brought me to this place of understanding, and I am so glad for it. So damn happy that I got divorced, lost my business, went bankrupt, because eventually, it brought me here, and here feels damn good. Joseph Citro says in, "Passing Strange," that "maybe our modern day Shamans serve to facilitate supernatural experiences. Maybe they serve as a gateway between the worlds." Talking to my childhood friend Steve Sousa, he would be inclined to agree with this. He thought that I was the one making stuff happen. "It always happened when you were around," was how he sweetly put it to me. Talking to other childhood friends, I know this isn't true, to a degree. The Siberians believed that the spirit world chose the Shaman and they wanted to have nothing to do with it. Because of the cost it made on them, it was only through a willingness to have the torment stop, that people became Shamans. Personally, this sounds like the story of my life, I know I was chosen for a reason. I am so thankful I was.

Map of Coggers

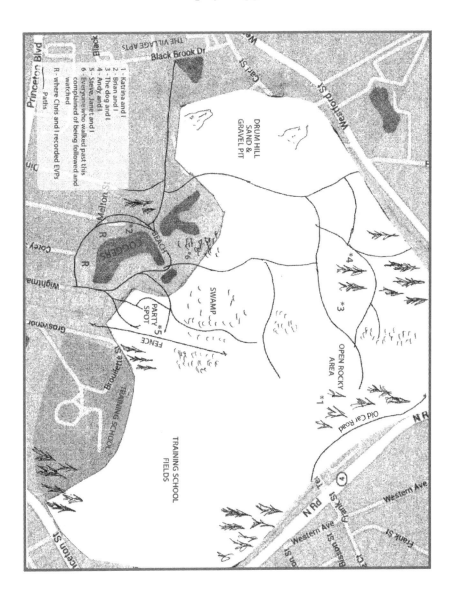

Made in the USA
Charleston, SC
18 June 2014